## HOLT

# Elements of Language

**FIRST COURSE**

# Chapter Tests in Standardized Test Formats

- Reading
- Writing
- Sentences and Paragraphs
- Grammar, Usage, Mechanics

**HOLT, RINEHART AND WINSTON**

A Harcourt Education Company

Orlando • **Austin** • New York • San Diego • London

ISBN 978-0-03-099312-1
ISBN 0-03-099312-1

1 2 3 4 5 6  018  13 12 11 10 09 08 07

# Table of Contents

# Table of Contents *(continued)*

## Communications

# Table of Contents *(continued)*

## Answer Sheets

# About These Tests

Every chapter in your *Elements of Language* Student Edition has an accompanying Chapter Test in a standardized test format. You will recognize the formats of a wide variety of standardized tests. The *Chapter Tests in Standardized Test Formats* will not only allow you to assess student performance, they will familiarize students with a range of standardized tests and give them practice in test-taking.

The Answer Keys for these tests are located on the *Teacher One Stop*™ **DVD-ROM with ExamView® Test Generator**.

**Part 1**
**Grammar, Usage, and Mechanics**

The Part 1 tests provide assessment for the rules and all key concepts taught in the grammar, usage, and mechanics chapters in the Student Edition. Students demonstrate their mastery of the instruction by answering multiple-choice items that test their knowledge of the content covered in the Student Edition.

**Part 2**
**Sentences and Paragraphs**

The Part 2 tests provide assessment for each major section within the Sentences and Paragraphs chapters. Students answer multiple-choice items about the content covered in the Student Edition. These items test students' mastery of the key concepts taught in the chapters.

**Part 3**
**Communications**

The Part 3 tests include assessment for both the Reading and the Writing Workshops. You may choose to administer the Reading and Writing Workshop tests separately or as one test after students have completed the chapter.

In the **Reading Workshop** test, students read a passage and respond to multiple-choice items. The passage is in the mode that students have just studied, and the multiple-choice items assess students' proficiency in the chapter's Reading Skill and Reading Focus.

The **Writing Workshop** test provides a passage containing problems or errors in several or all of the following areas: content, organization, style, grammar and usage, and mechanics. Students demonstrate their understanding of the mode of writing and their revising and proofreading skills by responding to multiple-choice items. Students identify elements of the mode of writing, restructure segments of the passage, add clarifying statements, refine language, and correct errors in the passage.

**Answer Sheets**

Answer sheets are provided in the back of the booklet. The answer sheets correspond to the letter answer options designated by a particular standardized test. Use the following chart to help you determine which answer sheet to use for each test. Students may use the **Correcting Common Errors Standardized Test Answer Sheet** for the **Grammar and Usage Test** and **Mechanics Test** in the Student Edition.

| Chapter | Answer Sheet |
|---|---|
| Chapters 1–16 | Answer Sheet 1 |
| Student Edition Chapter 17 | Common Errors Standardized Test Answer Sheet |
| Chapter 18 | Answer Sheet 3 |
| Chapter 19 | Answer Sheet 2 |
| Chapter 20: Reading Workshop | *Students answer on test.* |
| Writing Workshop | Answer Sheet 6 |
| Chapter 21: Reading Workshop | Answer Sheet 6 |
| Writing Workshop | Answer Sheet 6 |
| Chapter 22: Reading Workshop | Answer Sheet 4 |
| Writing Workshop | *Students answer on test.* |
| Chapter 23: Reading Workshop | Answer Sheet 5 |
| Writing Workshop | Answer Sheet 6 |
| Chapter 24: Reading Workshop | Answer Sheet 6 |
| Writing Workshop | Answer Sheet 4 |
| Chapter 25: Reading Workshop | Answer Sheet 6 |
| Writing Workshop | Answer Sheet 6 |
| Chapter 26: Reading Workshop | Answer Sheet 4 |
| Writing Workshop | *Students answer on test.* |

**Teacher One Stop™ DVD-ROM with ExamView® Test Generator**

All of the questions in this booklet are available on the *Teacher One Stop™* **DVD-ROM with ExamView® Test Generator.** Use the ExamView Test Generator to customize any of the tests in this booklet and create a test unique to your classroom situation. You can then print a test or post it to the *Holt Online Assessment* area at **my.hrw.com.**

**Holt Online Assessment**

*Holt Online Assessment* provides an easy way to administer tests to your students online. Students can log on to **my.hrw.com** to take a test that you have created using the ExamView Test Generator, or you can assign one of the tests already available on the site.

# The Sentence: Subject and Predicate, Kinds of Sentences

**DIRECTIONS** Read each sentence below. For items 1–6, choose the answer that identifies each underlined word or word group. For items 7–10, choose the answer that identifies the kind of sentence.

---

**EXAMPLES**

1. The fierce <u>rain</u> and howling <u>wind</u> drove us from our campsite.
   A complete subject
   B compound subject
   C simple predicate
   D compound verb

   Answer   (A)   **(B)**   (C)   (D)

2. Write your name in the upper right-hand corner.
   A interrogative
   B declarative
   C exclamatory
   D imperative

   Answer   (A)   (B)   (C)   **(D)**

---

1. <u>Each member of the team</u> scored in last night's game.
   A sentence
   B simple subject
   C complete subject
   D verb

2. Bianca <u>filled</u> the colorful piñata with fruit, nuts, and small toys.
   A verb
   B simple subject
   C compound verb
   D complete predicate

3. Either the rubber <u>duck</u> or the <u>mobile</u> would be a good gift for the baby.
   A compound subject
   B compound verb
   C complete subject
   D complete predicate

4. Jana <u>caught</u> the ball, <u>faked</u> to her left, and <u>dribbled</u> around the guard.
   A simple subject
   B complete predicate
   C compound subject
   D compound verb

**5.** <u>In many of his writings</u>, Abioseh Nicol <u>describes life in rural African villages</u>.
  A  complete subject
  B  complete predicate
  C  verb
  D  compound verb

**6.** Does your <u>salad</u> have onions in it?
  A  simple subject
  B  verb
  C  complete subject
  D  compound verb

**7.** Listen carefully to the flute solo in this song.
  A  exclamatory
  B  declarative
  C  imperative
  D  interrogative

**8.** Have you ever tasted Portuguese vegetable stew?
  A  imperative
  B  interrogative
  C  declarative
  D  exclamatory

**9.** I read that the jigsaw puzzle was invented as a game for teaching geography.
  A  declarative
  B  interrogative
  C  exclamatory
  D  imperative

**10.** What a great time we had at the amusement park!
  A  imperative
  B  declarative
  C  interrogative
  D  exclamatory

# Parts of Speech Overview: Noun, Pronoun, Adjective

**DIRECTIONS** Read each sentence below. Then, choose the answer that identifies each under-lined word or word group.

---

**EXAMPLE**

1. <u>This</u> laundry detergent has no dyes or perfumes.
   A abstract noun
   B demonstrative adjective
   C personal pronoun
   D proper noun

   Answer   (A)   (B)   (C)   (D)

---

1. My best <u>friend</u> wants to be a veterinarian.
   A common noun
   B proper noun
   C relative pronoun
   D article

2. Have <u>you</u> ever read this Korean folk tale?
   A compound noun
   B reflexive pronoun
   C personal pronoun
   D concrete noun

3. The <u>spicy</u> Mexican food is flavored with chili peppers.
   A indefinite pronoun
   B intensive pronoun
   C collective noun
   D adjective

4. Does this <u>footpath</u> lead to Balancing Rock?
   A proper noun
   B compound noun
   C reflexive pronoun
   D demonstrative adjective

5. The <u>crowd</u> cheered when Grandma received a gold medal in the Senior Olympics.
   A interrogative pronoun
   B compound noun
   C collective noun
   D proper adjective

6. Jerome Tiger is my favorite <u>American Indian</u> painter.
   A  article
   B  proper adjective
   C  demonstrative pronoun
   D  common noun

7. The colonists' desire for <u>freedom</u> led to war with Great Britain.
   A  abstract noun
   B  intensive pronoun
   C  collective noun
   D  adjective

8. After visiting the recycling plant, <u>everyone</u> in our class is eager to begin a school recycling program.
   A  indefinite pronoun
   B  demonstrative pronoun
   C  concrete noun
   D  article

9. The national bird of <u>Guatemala</u> is the colorful quetzal.
   A  collective noun
   B  proper adjective
   C  proper noun
   D  relative pronoun

10. <u>What</u> is the most effective search engine on the Internet?
   A  common noun
   B  adjective
   C  personal pronoun
   D  interrogative pronoun

# Parts of Speech Overview: Verb, Adverb, Preposition, Conjunction, Interjection

**DIRECTIONS** Read each sentence below. Then, choose the answer that identifies each underlined word or word group.

---

**EXAMPLE**

**1.** In the final seconds of the game, Cara <u>hit</u> a home run!
  **A** preposition
  **B** intransitive verb
  **C** adverb
  **D** transitive verb

  Answer

---

**1.** Giant pandas live in the bamboo forests <u>of</u> China.
  **A** verb
  **B** preposition
  **C** interjection
  **D** adverb

**2.** The beautiful waters of Tahiti attract swimmers <u>and</u> surfers from around the world.
  **A** preposition
  **B** helping verb
  **C** transitive verb
  **D** coordinating conjunction

**3.** Our teacher <u>read</u> aloud several poems by Countee Cullen.
  **A** action verb
  **B** linking verb
  **C** coordinating conjunction
  **D** correlative conjunction

**4.** Do you ever wonder where insects go <u>in the winter</u>?
  **A** verb phrase
  **B** prepositional phrase
  **C** interjection
  **D** linking verb

**5.** <u>Oh</u>! You've cleaned the entire house!

    **A** adverb

    **B** action verb

    **C** interjection

    **D** preposition

**6.** My favorite book <u>is</u> *Inspirations: Stories About Women Artists* by Leslie Sills.

    **A** linking verb

    **B** coordinating conjunction

    **C** preposition

    **D** action verb

**7.** Fascinated by the traditional Indian artwork, we <u>carefully</u> examined the yarn paintings, beadwork, and ceremonial bowls.

    **A** transitive verb

    **B** helping verb

    **C** interjection

    **D** adverb

**8.** My little sister wants to be <u>either</u> an astronaut <u>or</u> a ballerina when she grows up.

    **A** adverb

    **B** verb phrase

    **C** correlative conjunction

    **D** prepositional phrase

**9.** You <u>should eat</u> at least five servings of fruit and vegetables every day.

    **A** verb phrase

    **B** prepositional phrase

    **C** linking verb

    **D** adverb

**10.** Prem <u>will</u> teach us to play a form of volleyball that is popular in Thailand.

    **A** linking verb

    **B** adverb

    **C** helping verb

    **D** coordinating conjunction

# Complements: Direct and Indirect Objects, Subject Complements

**DIRECTIONS** Read each sentence below. Then, choose the answer that identifies each underlined word or word group according to its use in the sentence.

---

**EXAMPLE**

1. Angel Falls in Venezuela is the world's highest <u>waterfall</u>.
   A   direct object
   B   indirect object
   C   predicate nominative
   D   predicate adjective

   Answer   Ⓐ   Ⓑ   Ⓒ   Ⓓ

---

1. My great-aunt Ruby swims twenty <u>laps</u> every morning.
   A   predicate adjective
   B   direct object
   C   predicate nominative
   D   indirect object

2. To the travelers, the tropical air felt <u>hot</u> and <u>humid</u>.
   A   compound predicate nominative
   B   compound direct object
   C   compound indirect object
   D   compound predicate adjective

3. Michael offered <u>Nina</u> and <u>me</u> an Irish dish made with cabbage and mashed potatoes.
   A   compound indirect object
   B   compound predicate nominative
   C   compound predicate adjective
   D   compound direct object

4. In a backpack, each hiker carried <u>water</u>, <u>snacks</u>, and <u>sunscreen</u>.
   A   compound predicate adjective
   B   compound direct object
   C   compound predicate nominative
   D   compound indirect object

**5.** Was that <u>you</u> in the gorilla costume?
  **A**  direct object
  **B**  predicate nominative
  **C**  indirect object
  **D**  predicate adjective

**6.** A popular musical instrument in Zambia is the <u>drum</u>.
  **A**  predicate nominative
  **B**  predicate adjective
  **C**  direct object
  **D**  indirect object

**7.** Liang showed us a colorful <u>kite</u> and a paper <u>lantern</u> from China.
  **A**  compound indirect object
  **B**  compound predicate adjective
  **C**  compound predicate nominative
  **D**  compound direct object

**8.** Weren't you <u>exhausted</u> after yesterday's soccer game?
  **A**  predicate nominative
  **B**  direct object
  **C**  predicate adjective
  **D**  indirect object

**9.** The author and poet James Weldon Johnson also was a <u>songwriter</u>, <u>lawyer</u>, <u>educator</u>, and civil rights <u>leader</u>.
  **A**  compound direct object
  **B**  compound predicate nominative
  **C**  compound indirect object
  **D**  compound predicate adjective

**10.** Every Friday, Mrs. Zamora gives our <u>class</u> a free reading period.
  **A**  predicate adjective
  **B**  direct object
  **C**  indirect object
  **D**  predicate nominative

# The Phrase: Prepositional and Verbal Phrases

**DIRECTIONS** Read each sentence below. Then, identify the underlined word or phrase according to its use in the sentence.

---

**EXAMPLE**

1. Many of the beaches <u>of St. Kitts</u> have black, volcanic sand.
   A   infinitive
   B   prepositional phrase
   C   present participle
   D   infinitive phrase

   Answer   (A)   (B)   (C)   (D)

---

1. Many myths and legends are associated <u>with the moon</u>.
   A   adverb phrase
   B   adjective phrase
   C   participial phrase
   D   infinitive phrase

2. The <u>winning</u> goal was scored in the last few seconds of the game.
   A   infinitive
   B   adjective phrase
   C   participial phrase
   D   present participle

3. We gave the weary traveler a warm blanket and something <u>to eat</u>.
   A   past participle
   B   adverb phrase
   C   present participle
   D   infinitive

4. <u>Above the fireplace</u> hangs a painting by my great-grandmother.
   A   participial phrase
   B   adverb phrase
   C   infinitive phrase
   D   adjective phrase

5. The children believed that the map would lead them to a <u>buried</u> treasure.
   A  infinitive
   B  adjective phrase
   C  past participle
   D  present participle

6. Every September my family goes to Mexico <u>to celebrate Independence Day</u>.
   A  infinitive phrase
   B  past participle
   C  adjective phrase
   D  participial phrase

7. That beautiful bird <u>with a black hood</u> around its yellow face is a hooded warbler.
   A  adverb phrase
   B  present participle
   C  participial phrase
   D  adjective phrase

8. Have you ever heard of International Left-Handers Day, <u>celebrated on August 13</u>?
   A  present participle
   B  adverb phrase
   C  participial phrase
   D  infinitive

9. <u>To stay healthy</u>, I exercise, eat nutritious foods, and get plenty of rest.
   A  participial phrase
   B  present participle
   C  infinitive phrase
   D  adjective phrase

10. <u>Concentrating on the beat of the music</u>, the Zambian drummer danced across the stage.
   A  infinitive phrase
   B  adverb phrase
   C  participial phrase
   D  past participle

# The Clause: Independent and Subordinate Clauses

**DIRECTIONS** Read each sentence below. Then, choose the answer that identifies each under-lined word or word group.

---

**EXAMPLE**

  **1.** <u>If the telephone rings</u>, please answer it.
   **A**   independent clause
   **B**   adjective clause
   **C**   adverb clause
   **D**   not a clause

   Answer    (A)  (B)   **(C)**   (D)

---

**1.** Because she often felt tired, <u>Etta decided to include more fruits and vegetables in her diet</u>.
   **A**   adverb clause
   **B**   not a clause
   **C**   adjective clause
   **D**   independent clause

**2.** My uncle, <u>who has only one arm</u>, types on a special keyboard.
   **A**   adjective clause
   **B**   independent clause
   **C**   not a clause
   **D**   adverb clause

**3.** A collection of short stories <u>that you would enjoy reading</u> is *Many Thousand Gone: African Americans from Slavery to Freedom* by Virginia Hamilton.
   **A**   independent clause
   **B**   not a clause
   **C**   adjective clause
   **D**   adverb clause

**4.** You may talk quietly <u>until the show begins</u>.
   **A**   not a clause
   **B**   adjective clause
   **C**   independent clause
   **D**   adverb clause

**5.** On the Internet I learned about Peace Pals, <u>which focuses on people living in harmony with nature and with each other</u>.
   **A** independent clause
   **B** adverb clause
   **C** not a clause
   **D** adjective clause

**6.** <u>While Evelyn was in India</u>, she learned to make little clay lamps.
   **A** adverb clause
   **B** adjective clause
   **C** independent clause
   **D** not a clause

**7.** <u>In the Missouri River region the Cheyenne hunted buffalo</u>, which they used for food and clothing.
   **A** adjective clause
   **B** not a clause
   **C** adverb clause
   **D** independent clause

**8.** <u>About 75 percent of the world's fresh water</u> is frozen in glaciers.
   **A** not a clause
   **B** independent clause
   **C** adverb clause
   **D** adjective clause

**9.** <u>Did you know</u> that the fourteenth of July is Bastille Day in France?
   **A** adverb clause
   **B** adjective clause
   **C** independent clause
   **D** not a clause

**10.** The performers from Bali wear <u>beautiful costumes and play an orchestra of gongs, flutes, and drums</u>.
   **A** independent clause
   **B** not a clause
   **C** adjective clause
   **D** adverb clause

# Kinds of Sentence Structure: Simple, Compound, Complex, and Compound-Complex Sentences

**DIRECTIONS** Read each sentence below. Then, classify each sentence according to its structure.

---

**EXAMPLE**

**1.** The circus clown who is riding a unicycle is a very talented athlete.
   **A** simple sentence
   **B** compound-complex sentence
   **C** compound sentence
   **D** complex sentence

   Answer   (A)   (B)   (C)   (D)

---

**1.** I don't know Faith's e-mail address, but we can telephone her.
   **A** compound sentence
   **B** complex sentence
   **C** simple sentence
   **D** compound-complex sentence

**2.** The Kodo drummers from Sado Island in the Sea of Japan are amazing performers.
   **A** complex sentence
   **B** simple sentence
   **C** compound-complex sentence
   **D** compound sentence

**3.** Mary Helen has been practicing the violin solo that she will play in tonight's concert.
   **A** compound-complex sentence
   **B** simple sentence
   **C** compound sentence
   **D** complex sentence

**4.** When Jamal's family went to Kenya, they saw many game parks and beaches, but they spent most of their time with relatives in Nairobi.
   **A** complex sentence
   **B** compound-complex sentence
   **C** simple sentence
   **D** compound sentence

5. The actors on stage were confused, for they could not see their cue cards.
   A   simple sentence
   B   compound-complex sentence
   C   compound sentence
   D   complex sentence

6. In soups or in dips, yogurt is a part of almost every Armenian meal.
   A   simple sentence
   B   complex sentence
   C   compound sentence
   D   compound-complex sentence

7. Juggling is a popular hobby among the students at our school, but only a few of the teachers juggle.
   A   complex sentence
   B   compound-complex sentence
   C   simple sentence
   D   compound sentence

8. I feel better and look healthier when I exercise regularly.
   A   simple sentence
   B   complex sentence
   C   compound sentence
   D   compound-complex sentence

9. I have read several fairy-tale collections that include the Cinderella story, but my favorite is a book that belonged to my great-grandmother.
   A   compound-complex sentence
   B   simple sentence
   C   compound sentence
   D   complex sentence

10. Without anyone's help, Bill prepared dinner, served the meal, and washed the dishes.
   A   compound sentence
   B   compound-complex sentence
   C   simple sentence
   D   complex sentence

# Agreement: Subject and Verb, Pronoun and Antecedent

**DIRECTIONS** Read each set of sentences below. Three of the sentences in each set have errors in agreement; one sentence is written correctly. Choose the sentence that is written correctly, with NO ERRORS in agreement.

---

**EXAMPLE**

**1.** **A** Ima and her sister plays piano duets.
   **B** The committee differ in their opinions.
   **C** One of the award-winning poems were written by Joseph Bruchac.
   **D** The Marshall Islands are a chain of islands in the Pacific Ocean.

   Answer

---

**1.** **A** My grandmother and grandfather is competing in the marathon tomorrow.
   **B** An organic gardener don't use pesticides.
   **C** The brakes on my bicycle need adjustment.
   **D** Neither the cat nor her kittens has fleas.

**2.** **A** Party favors and a balloon were given to each child.
   **B** In Japan, doll festivals is held on March 3 and May 5.
   **C** Most of my friends likes country music.
   **D** Does veins or arteries carry blood from the heart to the rest of the body?

**3.** **A** Was both of the swimmers ready for the meet?
   **B** *Small Faces* are a collection of personal essays by Gary Soto.
   **C** Mathematics have always been my favorite subject.
   **D** Josh or Angelo will read his poem at tomorrow's assembly.

**4.** **A** That shirt don't match these pants.
   **B** Some of my relatives are going to Mecca, the birthplace of the prophet Mohammed.
   **C** Thirty minutes are a long time to wait for dinner.
   **D** A flashing light or a colorful sign indicate the store's featured items.

**5.** **A** The tall reeds along the water's edge shelters the ducklings.
   **B** Everyone on the nature walk brought his or her camera.
   **C** An apple or some raisins is a good choice for a snack.
   **D** Isn't most Turkish rugs made from sheep's wool?

**6.** **A** Today our class votes on a new school motto.
   **B** The beads in my Nigerian necklace is made of polished glass and colored stones.
   **C** There's over twenty participants in the skateboard competition.
   **D** Kay or her brother deliver the morning newspaper.

**7.** **A** One of Faith Ringgold's story quilts show the rooftop of a city apartment building.

**B** Neither the coach nor the fans agrees with the referee's call.

**C** Don't this fresh carrot juice taste delicious?

**D** Both of my young cousins enjoy picture books by Mitsumasa Anno.

**8.** **A** Nobody in the advanced drama classes have performed in a musical.

**B** Edena, Delores, or Susan score most of our team's goals.

**C** My best friend and neighbor, Rafael, tells me stories of his childhood in Puerto Rico.

**D** Someone left their sheet music on the piano stool.

**9.** **A** Ten thousand dollars were donated to a local charity.

**B** Heart disease and cancer is related to diets high in fat.

**C** Under the sofa cushion are an earring and a gold button.

**D** The Austin Writers' League are sponsoring a short-story contest.

**10.** **A** Measles occur most commonly in childhood.

**B** Each of the girls do volunteer work in their spare time.

**C** Either Chile or Brazil use the peso as their currency.

**D** At the fiesta, one of the most popular masked dances features a tiger.

# Using Verbs Correctly: Principal Parts, Regular and Irregular Verbs, Tense, Voice

**DIRECTIONS** Read each set of sentences below. Three of the sentences in each set have errors in verb usage; one sentence is written correctly. Choose the sentence that is written correctly, with NO ERRORS in verb usage.

---

**EXAMPLE**

**1.** **A** Sit your fishing gear in the back of the boat.
**B** When I looked out the airplane window, I see the blue Caribbean waters.
**C** We climbed to the top of the Empire State Building.
**D** While visiting India, Jill drunk buffalo milk.

Answer

---

**1.** **A** I done twenty sit-ups before breakfast.
**B** Susan told us a Russian folk tale she learned from her grandmother.
**C** The bee drinks the flower's nectar and made honey.
**D** Is steam rising from the soup kettle?

**2.** **A** Please sit the groceries on the kitchen table.
**B** For the kite festival, Jiro and his cousins are building a box kite.
**C** Aunt Dana has already ran three marathons this year.
**D** When I went to the art gallery, I see paintings by Jacob Lawrence.

**3.** **A** The price of bread has risen since last summer.
**B** Nabela feeded camels at the new petting zoo.
**C** Blain hurted his knee when he fell from the balance beam.
**D** Where has Dad lain his keys?

**4.** **A** I have wrote two letters to my pen pal in Taiwan.
**B** This is the third year that Grandma has raced in the Owensville Lawn Mower Race.
**C** Our dog has laid in Mom's herb garden.
**D** My little sister drawed a colorful picture of the food pyramid.

**5.** **A** I have choosed a collection of Hungarian folk tales as our club's next discussion book.
**B** The soldiers raised their country's flag during the parade.
**C** We have ask Mara about her rafting adventure.
**D** Has the bell rang for class to begin?

**6.** **A** I am laying your clean clothes on the bed.
**B** Are you sitting the party favors by each place at the table?
**C** Have you ever ate these fruit-filled Vietnamese cakes?
**D** Our team has broke several swim-meet records today.

**7.** **A**  This morning I seen a Carolina wren at the bird feeder.

  **B**  When we visit my cousin in Portugal, we saw cork oak trees.

  **C**  A nurse has spoke to our class about the importance of eating nutritious foods.

  **D**  The Nigerian dancer raised his drum in the air.

**8.** **A**  Celine Dion sung the theme song from *Titanic.*

  **B**  We have been setting in this waiting room long enough.

  **C**  Is the baby lying on a lambskin pad?

  **D**  Logan has rose before dawn every day this week.

**9.** **A**  Eli is wearing his new contact lenses today.

  **B**  Laying down is not the best treatment for most back pain.

  **C**  When I sing in the shower, I sometimes sang off key.

  **D**  The parachute is suppose to open when you pull the cord.

**10.** **A**  The wool sweater has shrank from being washed in hot water.

  **B**  On the top bunk laid Jim's cat, Ernie.

  **C**  At the community center, Devon has been taking a class for baby sitters.

  **D**  Without sheet music, Hector sits down at the piano and played a Bulgarian folk song.

# Using Pronouns Correctly: Nominative and Objective Case Forms

**DIRECTIONS** Read each set of sentences below. Three of the sentences in each set have errors in pronoun usage; one sentence is written correctly. Choose the sentence that is written correctly, with NO ERRORS in pronoun usage.

---

**EXAMPLE**

**1. A** The winners of the math contest are they.
  **B** For the picture, will you sit on the tree limb above Steve and he?
  **C** Just ask we coaches if you have a question.
  **D** Him and me will groom the horses after our ride.

Answer  (A) (B) (C) (D)

---

**1. A** You and her can finish the experiment tomorrow.
  **B** Mr. Lambe hired we boys for weekend yardwork.
  **C** The doctor showed me the X-ray of my broken wrist.
  **D** Did the children play by theirselves most of the morning?

**2. A** Ved told Sara and we about *Divali*, India's festival of lights.
  **B** The children held hands and formed a circle around she and I.
  **C** Whom is that girl in the pink hat?
  **D** My favorite movie stars are Leonardo DiCaprio and he.

**3. A** The camp counselors seemed to enjoy theirselves at the talent show.
  **B** Grandma and her are singing a duet in the talent contest.
  **C** For breakfast, Carlos will make Tina and I a Mexican egg dish called *huevos rancheros*.
  **D** To whom did you lend your book?

**4. A** Will you tell him and me about your trip to the Netherlands?
  **B** Mom and me built a greenhouse to protect the plants from wind and frost.
  **C** Before each race, Carl asks hisself, "Can I do better than the last time?"
  **D** Natalie wants to ride with Brad and I.

**5. A** Delia and us designed the costumes for the school play.
  **B** For whom did Grandpa paint the picture?
  **C** The featured musicians are her and Yo-Yo Ma.
  **D** At what age will the baby be able to feed hisself?

**6. A** Us honor students would like to tutor after school.
  **B** Will you please take Alana and I to the mall?
  **C** Those copies of Julia Alvarez's latest book were reserved for Marta and me.
  **D** Her and her family do volunteer work at the animal shelter every Saturday.

**7.** A  The next band to perform should be we.
    B  On Saturdays us swimmers spend the whole day at the pool.
    C  During spring break, Chun-Hyang and them painted the garage.
    D  The park ranger gave Mike and I a map.

**8.** A  Before going onstage, us dancers listened for our cue.
    B  Whom will you ask to sponsor the dance?
    C  We chose Misako and she as class representatives.
    D  Sue and them planted flowers in front of the school.

**9.** A  It must have been he on the telephone.
    B  Whom will be the first to tell a tall tale?
    C  Without Shada and she, our team has little hope of winning.
    D  When will us seventh-graders get to tour the state capitol building?

**10.** A  Just between you and I, your essay needs a little more work.
    B  Among the recent winners of the middle school poetry prize are Charles Guerrero, Arthurine Jackson, and she.
    C  Who did you choose as your lab partner?
    D  The top scorers in today's game were Mary Helen and me.

for **CHAPTER 11** | *pages 264–285*                                   **CHAPTER TEST**

# Using Modifiers Correctly: Comparison and Placement

**DIRECTIONS** Read each set of sentences below. Three of the sentences in each set have errors in modifier usage; one sentence is written correctly. Choose the sentence that is written correctly, with NO ERRORS in modifier usage.

---
**EXAMPLE**

**1. A** Blaine swims more faster than I do.
   **B** After reading all of the nonsense poems, decide which one is sillier.
   **C** Waiting for the movie to begin, the theater was crowded and noisy.
   **D** My aunt, who uses a wheelchair, has redesigned her kitchen to be barrier-free.

Answer

---

**1. A** I've never seen the soccer team play so good together.
   **B** The Lithuanian potato dumplings tasted deliciously.
   **C** Confused, I asked for a map of the mall stores.
   **D** Did you see the trophies that Grandma won in the attic?

**2. A** The bicycle has a basket for books that she rides to school.
   **B** When the guest speaker approached the microphone, the audience became quiet.
   **C** I don't know no one who can restore old photographs as well as she can.
   **D** We saw many beautiful wildflowers hiking through the woods.

**3. A** A cheetah can run more swiftly than a zebra.
   **B** Can you speak Spanish as good as your sister?
   **C** The book *The Clay Marble* describes peace and friendship in the midst of war by Minfong Ho.
   **D** Chuck didn't want nobody to help him with his project.

**4. A** Our clay sculptures turned out good.
   **B** The most largest country in South America is Brazil.
   **C** The dogwood trees attracted beautiful, light-blue butterflies that we planted in our backyard.
   **D** This is director Steven Spielberg's most famous movie.

**5. A** I looked in an old mirror to fix my hair, which had begun to crack.
   **B** Although he does not practice every day, Paul can play the piano very well.
   **C** Of the three costume designs, this is the better one.
   **D** That burnt food smells badly!

**6. A** Tired but proud, the children finally finished cleaning the garage.
   **B** At tonight's recital we hope to dance as good as we did at rehearsal.
   **C** Saul likes Armenian flat bread more better than he likes flour tortillas.
   **D** Of the two girls, Joan throws the ball farthest.

**7.** **A** Leon feels nervously about giving his oral report.

 **B** The most easiest way to get to the island is by ferry.

 **C** Singing "It's a Small World," joyful children filled the stadium.

 **D** I can't hardly walk today because I'm sore from yesterday's karate class.

**8.** **A** A carved mask hangs above our fireplace from the island of Puerto Rico.

 **B** This football is the less expensive of the two.

 **C** Although I've been introduced to him several times, I can't never remember his name.

 **D** Don't the stars look brightly tonight?

**9.** **A** Winding colorful yarn around crossed popsicle sticks, we made "gods' eyes," an American Indian craft.

 **B** In 1997, fourteen-year-old Tara Lipinski became the most youngest skater in history to win the World Figure Skating Championships.

 **C** Startled, the noise made him jump.

 **D** Look at the race car on the track that has a bright red spoiler!

**10.** **A** There isn't hardly any window cleaner left.

 **B** Miss Silko showed us the artistic sculptures and temples of Cambodia using slides and color photos.

 **C** A dog without a collar appeared at our front door.

 **D** Lying in my tent, the night sounds were comforting.

# A Glossary of Usage: Common Usage Problems

**DIRECTIONS** Read each set of sentences below. Three of the sentences in each set have errors in formal, standard usage; one sentence is written correctly. Choose the sentence that is written correctly, with NO ERRORS in formal, standard usage.

> **EXAMPLE**
>
>   **1.**  **A**   Are we allowed to ride our bicycles anywheres in the park?
>          **B**   The hikers didn't have hardly any water left at the end of the day.
>          **C**   We divided the duties equally among all the club members.
>          **D**   Shel Silverstein was an author which also illustrated his books.
>
>   Answer   

**1.**  **A**   We ain't quite ready to give our demonstration.
     **B**   Now that I'm older, I like spicy food some.
     **C**   You're report on "Women's Firsts" was fantastic!
     **D**   Doesn't Nicholas Payton play the trumpet well?

**2.**  **A**   The softball sailed over the fence and busted a window.
     **B**   This type of Belgian lace is made in Brussels.
     **C**   I can't go to the movies without I clean my room first.
     **D**   Josh voted for hisself in the class election.

**3.**  **A**   When you go to dance class, take your tap shoes.
     **B**   How come clouds are different shapes?
     **C**   Uncle Francis is learning me an Italian song from Tuscany.
     **D**   Belinda lives a long ways from here.

**4.**  **A**   Who's sweater is in my locker?
     **B**   I liked the book more than I liked the movie.
     **C**   Jóhannes Kjarval he was one of Iceland's most popular painters.
     **D**   You had ought to learn to sew on a button.

**5.**  **A**   The alligator snapping turtle can shut it's jaws with great force.
     **B**   Dwayne listens to a lot of reggae music.
     **C**   I read in the newspaper where the community pool is closed for repairs.
     **D**   This here book was signed by the author Virginia Hamilton.

**6.**  **A**   They're traveling to Western Samoa this summer to visit their relatives.
     **B**   How many of them stamp albums belonged to your grandfather?
     **C**   Uncle Ahmed told us a Algerian folk tale.
     **D**   Josephine is real interested in world mythology.

7.  **A**  Where are my headphones at?
    **B**  *Semaphore* is when two flags or two flashlights are used for sending messages.
    **C**  I will try and beat the school record in today's race.
    **D**  It's always exciting to learn something new!

8.  **A**  Did you really get to go inside of the governor's office?
    **B**  I used to baby-sit my twin cousins.
    **C**  When I was in New York, I could of visited the National Museum of the American Indian.
    **D**  The astronauts are already for takeoff.

9.  **A**  Please try to get home in time for supper.
    **B**  You look like you know the answer, Tommy.
    **C**  The leftover sandwich tasted badly.
    **D**  I stayed up real late to finish my science project.

10. **A**  We're not sure why less people came to the concert this year.
    **B**  I have been practicing every day, like my piano teacher suggested.
    **C**  Elayne fell while water-skiing, but she seems all right now.
    **D**  Everyone accept Burt has read Lensey Namioka's book *The Coming of the Bear*.

# Capital Letters: Rules for Capitalization

**DIRECTIONS** Read each set of sentences below. Three of the sentences in each set have errors in capitalization; one sentence is written correctly. Choose the sentence that is written correctly, with NO ERRORS in capitalization.

---

**EXAMPLE**

**1. A**  Doesn't jerome b. knowles have a great storytelling style?
  **B**  half of my weekly allowance goes into my college fund.
  **C**  Baskets, baked clay pots, masks, and shields are among the crafts for sale in the marketplace.
  **D**  How exciting that aunt Edith is going on a safari!

  Answer

---

**1. A**  do you take medication for your allergies?
  **B**  In nigeria, we met Rhonda's uncle George.
  **C**  Thick clouds cover the surface of venus.
  **D**  Shouldn't I brush and floss my teeth at least twice a day?

**2. A**  There are three major rivers in the country of senegal.
  **B**  Many koreans eat *kimchi,* a popular side dish made of pickled vegetables and spices.
  **C**  When should I light the candles on the dinner table?
  **D**  Do you have a schwinn® bicycle?

**3. A**  Kenai Fjords National Park in Alaska is a breeding place for many birds.
  **B**  The president is aboard *air force one* flying to Japan.
  **C**  Ponga attends the university of zambia in the city of Lusaka.
  **D**  My family fasts on the Jewish holiday yom kippur.

**4. A**  We decided to name our class's literary magazine *a different view.*
  **B**  The Congressional Medal of Honor is the highest U.S. military award.
  **C**  Does the community college offer a chinese cooking class?
  **D**  Please take the orange juice and box of kleenex® tissue to Aunt Dorothy.

**5. A**  One of the most beautiful buildings in the world is the taj mahal in India.
  **B**  I hope someday to see the Alvin Ailey American Dance Theater perform.
  **C**  In the school newspaper Kiki reviewed Sonia Levitin's book *the return.*
  **D**  The elegant costume was made of thai silk.

**6. A**  Our school celebrates Arbor Day by planting trees throughout the city.
  **B**  According to legend, Hiawatha was a powerful chieftain of the iroquois.
  **C**  I can't remember who won the spingarn medal last year.
  **D**  Isn't this booklet published by the american heart association?

**7.** **A**  Iris won the geography contest by naming kathmandu as the capital of nepal.

  **B**  The national museum of african art displays art made of many materials such as wood, metal, and ceramic.

  **C**  One of the most widely practiced religions in Vietnam is buddhism.

  **D**  The secretary of commerce called an emergency meeting.

**8.** **A**  Did king Fahd rule Saudi Arabia during the Persian Gulf War?

  **B**  In England, people celebrate shrove tuesday by eating pancakes.

  **C**  Since Grandpa Williams retired from teaching, he has spent much of his free time volunteering at the elementary school.

  **D**  I finished my Algebra homework before supper.

**9.** **A**  When did the first woman compete against men in an international surfing contest?

  **B**  Aunt Eliza said, "the family reunion will be held next weekend."

  **C**  Did this film win a prize at the cannes film festival?

  **D**  Our art appreciation II class is going on a field trip to a local art museum.

**10.** **A**  I invited my Cousin Juan to the party.

  **B**  Have you read general Colin Powell's autobiography *My American Journey*?

  **C**  Several members of the space shuttle *Columbia* researched the effects of weightlessness on blood pressure.

  **D**  For centuries, travelers have been guided by the star polaris, which always shines in the northern sky.

# Punctuation: End Marks, Commas, Semicolons, and Colons

**DIRECTIONS** Read each set of sentences below. Three of the sentences in each set have errors in punctuation; one sentence is written correctly. Choose the sentence that is written correctly, with NO ERRORS in punctuation.

---

**EXAMPLE**

  **1.**  **A**   On our vacation to Yellowstone National Park we saw mountains rivers, and wildflowers.

       **B**   The jaguar, which is hunted for its skin, is becoming rare.

       **C**   Carl is visiting his aunt in St Louis Missouri.

       **D**   My sister Sonia was born on February 8 1995.

      Answer   Ⓐ      Ⓒ   Ⓓ

---

**1.**  **A**   Please close the door.

     **B**   Will you make me a sandwich.

     **C**   What an amazing concert that was.

     **D**   I usually shower in the evening?

**2.**  **A**   On July 27 1999, our family moved to Ft. Worth, Texas.

     **B**   Send your letter to 124 Stone Street Durham North Carolina.

     **C**   Joan received a postcard from her pen pal in Frankfurt, Germany.

     **D**   Sandra Cisneros was born in Chicago Illinois, in 1954.

**3.**  **A**   We visited Lyndon B Johnson's home in Johnson City Texas.

     **B**   Did you know Sara that the author Jean Fritz spent her childhood in China?

     **C**   In Lancaster Pa. we visited an Amish community.

     **D**   A. B. Guthrie wrote stories about the West.

**4.**  **A**   We still have Monday Tuesday and Wednesday to do our work.

     **B**   The thin, lumpy cake layers were disappointing.

     **C**   How beautiful that sunset is.

     **D**   Len washed dried, and chopped tomatoes for the salad.

**5.**  **A**   We need of course a backup plan.

     **B**   You would enjoy reading this book, I believe.

     **C**   Anchorage the biggest city in Alaska is our destination.

     **D**   Will you be able to join us Rudy?

**6.**  **A**   I read an article on modern Egypt, and I wrote a report on what I learned.

     **B**   Frightened by the dogs the cat climbed higher in the tree.

     **C**   Theo wants a ferret but his apartment complex doesn't allow pets.

     **D**   Yesterday, my friend offered me a ride to the library and I accepted gladly.

7.  **A** Our family always eats supper at 6:00 P.M.
    **B** Yes I can see the Big Dipper in the sky.
    **C** Why we didn't expect you until tomorrow!
    **D** The astronomy lecture begins promptly at 8:00 P.M.

8.  **A** To make that bread, you need the following yeast, flour, and honey.
    **B** Elephants are vegetarians, they eat grasses leaves, fruit, and small branches.
    **C** The following students received awards: Tonya, Armando, Leon, and Theresa.
    **D** The killer whale is a large powerful mammal.

9.  **A** William Travis commanded the men at the Alamo; Davy Crockett and James Bowie were his aides.
    **B** This morning I made my lunch then I forgot to bring it.
    **C** Rabbits have been eating our crops, we put a fake snake in the garden to scare the rabbits away.
    **D** Joey drew a line in the dirt, we pitched horseshoes from behind the line.

10. **A** Poaching in Africa is widespread many wild animals are hunted for meat or for trophies.
    **B** The coat of the polar bear, which varies from pure white to shades of yellow, blends in with the snow.
    **C** Magda my neighbor was born in Mexico City.
    **D** Making a desk for my room we cut the wood sanded it, and applied a wax finish.

# Punctuation: Underlining (Italics), Quotation Marks, Apostrophes, Hyphens, Parentheses, Brackets, and Dashes

**DIRECTIONS** Read each set of sentences below. Three of the sentences in each set have errors in punctuation; one sentence is written correctly. Choose the sentence that is written correctly, with NO ERRORS in punctuation.

---

**EXAMPLE**

**1. A** Is *supersede* the only English word that ends in *–sede*?
   **B** The cities mayors agreed to meet again in May.
   **C** "In our yard," said Adrian, we've made a compost heap from vegetable scraps, leaves, and grass clippings."
   **D** Rene announced, "Anna plays in the final round of the chess tournament tomorrow".

   Answer

---

**1. A** I just read a great book called Somewhere in the Darkness by Walter Dean Myers.
   **B** Fold your ballots in half after voting, instructed the poll worker.
   **C** Is this bracelet your's?
   **D** This recipe calls for one-half cup of milk.

**2. A** The police officer inquired, "Are you familiar with the helmet law for cyclists"?
   **B** In the story Amigo Brothers by Piri Thomas, two best friends compete for the same prize.
   **C** How many *a*'s are in the word *aardvark*?
   **D** I think youll like this Celtic music.

**3. A** The items that sold well at my familys garage sale were toys, clothes, comics, books, and furniture.
   **B** I found somebody's address book in the cafeteria.
   **C** James Naismith 1861–1939 invented the game of basketball.
   **D** "All hands on deck." shouted the captain.

**4. A** Country singer LeAnn Rimes I know this seems unbelievable began singing before she was two years old!
   **B** "Have you ever tasted *gnocchi*?" asked Eva. "They are small Italian dumplings."
   **C** Because I groom my dogs coat often, it is clean and glossy.
   **D** The salesperson said, "With this software you can create greeting cards"

**5. A** "My family celebrates Kwanzaa each year", explained Jerome.
   **B** Anyone's painting could win first prize.
   **C** "Your skin," said the nurse "protects your internal organs and controls body temperature."
   **D** I have been practicing the correct use of the words learn and teach.

**6.** **A**   Among the artist Bill Reids bronze sculptures is *Spirit of Haida Gwaii.*

    **B**   After tearing apart an anthill with its strong claws, an anteater can catch hundreds of ants at a time with its thin, sticky tongue.

    **C**   Our classroom seems noisier than theirs.'

    **D**   "English and Chinese are the official languages of Hong Kong." said Anita.

**7.** **A**   "What time will Grandma's performance begin" asked John?

    **B**   At the Earth Day celebration I read the Anna Lee Walters poem I Am of the Earth.

    **C**   We will get several doctor's opinions before making a decision.

    **D**   Your lowercase *n*'s and *h*'s look very similar.

**8.** **A**   Leo read thirty five books during his summer vacation.

    **B**   "Did Coach Snelling really say, "We have the best team in the state"?" asked Diego.

    **C**   Vietnamese people often use *nuoc nam*—it's a fish sauce—to flavor their food.

    **D**   I cant wait to see the pictures you took at the party!

**9.** **A**   Our citys efforts to reduce water pollution have been successful.

    **B**   What did the camp director mean when she said, "Bring only the necessary equipment"?

    **C**   The television program The Living Edens explores some of the most beautiful natural spaces on earth.

    **D**   Directions to the park appear later in this booklet. (See page 8 illustration 2 for a map.)

**10.** **A**   The longest river in Lithuania is the Neman called Nemunas in Lithuanian.

    **B**   In your beach bag, always be sure to pack drinking water, towels, magazines, sun -glasses, and sunscreen.

    **C**   Craig explained, "When the performer said, 'Keep the music alive in your heart,' the audience cheered."

    **D**   Are landfills or incinerators better for the disposal of trash? asked Nathan.

# Spelling: Improving Your Spelling

**DIRECTIONS** Read each set of sentences below. The underlined word is spelled incorrectly in three of the sentences in each set; in one of the sentences, the underlined word is spelled correctly. Choose the sentence in which the underlined word is spelled CORRECTLY.

---
**EXAMPLE**

1. **A**  The temperature dropped ten <u>degrees</u> in the last hour!
   **B**  Wear slippers if your <u>feets</u> are cold.
   **C**  He baked two <u>loafs</u> of pumpernickel bread.
   **D**  Nearly half the world's <u>sheeps</u> are bred for their fine wool.

   Answer  (A)  (B)  (C)  (D)
---

1. **A**  Please be <u>quite</u> during the film.
   **B**  I <u>misunderstood</u> your directions.
   **C**  Has Hana <u>shone</u> you her Japanese paper lantern?
   **D**  We can offer the stray kitten a <u>loveing</u> home.

2. **A**  We need warm <u>clothes</u> for winter camping.
   **B**  Grandma claims that her <u>dayly</u> swim keeps her healthy.
   **C**  Twelve <u>inchs</u> equal one foot.
   **D**  Our Boy Scout troop collected ten boxes of <u>toyes</u> for the children's hospital.

3. **A**  I am <u>truely</u> sorry if I hurt your feelings.
   **B**  Juan has scored more points <u>then</u> Mike has.
   **C**  To breed, many <u>fishs</u> migrate from salt water to fresh water.
   **D**  Mr. Kerns needs help <u>carrying</u> his groceries to the car, Jimmy.

4. **A**  Wear <u>lose</u>, comfortable clothing to dance class.
   **B**  We found a <u>mysteryous</u> message in a bottle.
   **C**  Our <u>grandfathers</u> both volunteer at the school library.
   **D**  <u>Whose</u> playing first base?

5. **A**  My favorite short <u>storys</u> are written by Gary Soto.
   **B**  How many Texas governors have been <u>women</u>?
   **C**  Walking <u>threw</u> the snow was difficult.
   **D**  Our blackberry <u>bushs</u> are loaded with fruit.

**6.** **A** Mother keeps her sharp <u>knifes</u> in the kitchen drawer.

    **B** We <u>past</u> several roadside fruit stands on our way to the farm.

    **C** A snake often sheds <u>its</u> skin in one piece.

    **D** Is it better to stretch before or after <u>runing</u>?

**7.** **A** <u>Bananas</u> are a good source of vitamin $B_6$, potassium, and magnesium.

    **B** We must avoid <u>waisting</u> our natural resources.

    **C** Is Ghana one of the <u>countrys</u> that borders the Ivory Coast?

    **D** Sit-ups can help strengthen <u>week</u> abdominal muscles.

**8.** **A** One of Japan's more popular <u>amusment</u> parks is Huis ten Bosch.

    **B** His report was <u>breif</u> but interesting.

    **C** Daytime temperatures in the <u>dessert</u> can reach 131°F in the shade.

    **D** We watched two <u>videos</u> about scuba diving.

**9.** **A** For the salsa I need onions, cilantro, and fresh <u>tomatos</u>.

    **B** A positive attitude can help you to <u>succede</u>.

    **C** "Are you <u>disatisfied</u> with the service?" asked the restaurant manager.

    **D** The school <u>counselor</u> encouraged Nathan to enroll in art classes.

**10.** **A** One of Tanzania's <u>cheif</u> foods is a porridge called *ugali*.

    **B** Does the word *mammal* have three <u>*m's*</u>?

    **C** The "Happy Birthday" banner will be most <u>noticable</u> above the door.

    **D** Uncle Rico and his two <u>brother-in-laws</u> are writing a family cookbook.

# Correcting Common Errors: Key Language Skills Review

**DIRECTIONS** Read each set of sentences. Three of the sentences in each set contain common errors in language skills; one sentence is written correctly. Choose the sentence that is written correctly, with NO ERRORS in language skills.

---

**EXAMPLE**

**1.** **A** One of my favorite books is "Rice Without Rain" by Minfong Ho.
   **B** Weve been waiting for an hour to buy tickets.
   **C** One of my sister's favorite games is lacrosse.
   **D** "Did anyone call"? asked Mara.

   Answer

---

**1.** **A** When my great-grandparents came to the United States.
   **B** A dreidel is a spinning top used in a Hanukkah game.
   **C** Our family planted an herb garden the basil and rosemary are growing quickly.
   **D** Accepted a baby-sitting job in our neighborhood.

**2.** **A** This shelf of books is arranged in alphabetical order.
   **B** Neither of our dogs like getting a bath.
   **C** In the exhibit is two paintings by William H. Johnson.
   **D** Either the coach or her assistants gives a halftime pep talk.

**3.** **A** Everyone must clean up their own campsite.
   **B** Either Ana or Jane will read their poem first.
   **C** My little brother and his friend always share their toys.
   **D** The Peace Corps has their national headquarters in Washington, D.C.

**4.** **A** Have you ate at least five servings of fruits and vegetables today?
   **B** When the phone rang, Bill answers it.
   **C** Jean Driscoll, an athlete who uses a wheelchair, has spoke at a school assembly.
   **D** Please lie down and rest for a while.

**5.** **A** Him and me visited the Metropolitan Museum of Art's Web site.
   **B** Us students want to know more about kachina dolls.
   **C** You may sit between Kiri and I.
   **D** Whom have they chosen as captain?

**6.** **A** Of the two games, checkers is easier to play.
   **B** Sita performed good in her first piano recital.
   **C** I hardly know nothing about the Hopi culture.
   **D** The package belongs to Aretha wrapped in silver paper.

**7. A** I should of warmed up before the race.

   **B** With a proud smile, Abdullah accepted the award.

   **C** Less people live in Argentina than in Brazil.

   **D** Their planning a surprise party for Uncle Leo.

**8. A** When I get home from school, Mother always asks, "what did you learn today?"

   **B** Are we having a test in History class tomorrow?

   **C** Mae C. Jemison was the first African American woman to travel to outer space.

   **D** In the book *the Magic Listening Cap*, Yoshiko Uchida tells fourteen Japanese folk tales.

**9. A** Elton has lived in Phoenix, Arizona; Mexico City, Mexico; Los Angeles, California; and Lima, Peru.

   **B** If a starfish loses an arm the arm gradually grows back.

   **C** Van Thang offered us a Vietnamese pickled-pork snack called *nem* but we were not hungry.

   **D** To make rakhi bracelets, you will need: colored cardboard, large buttons, sequins, and ribbons.

**10. A** Michelangelo painted beautiful pictures on the Sistine Chapel cieling.

   **B** Watch this quarter disappear!

   **C** Leah has been writing to a pen pal in Mongolia.

   **D** Our school cafeteria offers baked potatos for lunch every day.

# Writing Effective Sentences

**DIRECTIONS** Read each passage. Then read each question after the passage. Choose the best answer. Then mark the space for the answer you have chosen.

## Boosters Host Sale

On Wednesday, March 29, a bake sale will be held. The Booster Club will hold the bake sale. Proceeds to the girls' soccer team. In April, put on your kneepads. The Annual All-School Skate is on Saturday, April 22. All students, their families, and guests. All are invited. Anyone who brings a can of food for the food drive will be admitted for half price, the food will go to the Logan County Food Pantry. Proceeds from this event will be divided among all clubs. The clubs are the extracurricular activity clubs.

**1** **How can the first two sentences best be combined?**

A   On Wednesday, March 29, a bake sale will be held and by the Booster Club.

B   The Booster Club, on Wednesday, March 29, will hold a bake sale.

C   On Wednesday, March 29, a bake sale will be held, and the Booster Club will hold the bake sale.

D   On Wednesday, March 29, the Booster Club will hold a bake sale.

**2** **Which of the following is a fragment?**

A   Proceeds to the girls' soccer team.

B   In April, put on your kneepads.

C   The Annual All-School Skate is on Saturday, April 22.

D   Proceeds from this event will be divided among all clubs.

**3** 

> All students, their families, and guests.

**What would be the best way to revise this sentence fragment?**

A   Add a verb.

B   Combine it with the previous sentence.

C   Combine it with the following sentence.

D   *It does not need to be revised.*

**4** 

> Anyone who brings a can of food for the food drive will be admitted for half price, the food will go to the Logan County Food Pantry.

**This is an example of a —**

A   stringy sentence

B   sentence fragment

C   run-on sentence

D   wordy sentence

**5** 

> Proceeds from this event will be divided among all clubs. The clubs are the extracurricular activity clubs.

**What would be the best way to combine these sentences?**

A   Proceeds from this event will be divided among all clubs, the clubs are the extracurricular activity clubs.

B   Proceeds from this event will be divided among all clubs, and the clubs are the extracurricular ones.

C   Proceeds from this event will be divided among all clubs if the clubs are the extracurricular activity clubs.

D   Proceeds from this event will be divided among all extracurricular activity clubs.

## Jesse Owens Wins Gold

Jesse Owens was a great runner. He set several world records. Owens went to Ohio, and he went to high school in Ohio, and his classmates realized that he could run fast. Then in college, everyone knew. At Ohio State University, Owens set three records in one day. The records were world records. A year later, in 1936, the Olympic games were held in Berlin, Germany. Jesse Owens ran for the United States. He also jumped for the United States. Earned four gold medals. One record he set at those Olympic Games stood for twenty-five years.

 **6**

> Jesse Owens was a great runner. He set several world records.

**What would be the best way to combine these sentences?**

A   Jesse Owens was a great runner, and he set several world records.

B   Jesse Owens was a great runner who set several world records.

C   Jesse Owens, setting several world records, was a great runner.

D   Jesse Owens set several world records, and he was a great runner.

 **7**

> At Ohio State University, Owens set three records in one day. The records were world records.

**What would be the best way to combine these sentences?**

A   At Ohio State University, Owens set three world records in one day.

B   At Ohio State University, Owens set three records in one day. They were world records.

C   For world records, Owens set three records in one day at Ohio State University.

D   At Ohio State University, Owens set three records in one day, and the records were world records.

 **8**

> Owens went to Ohio, and he went to high school in Ohio, and his classmates realized he could run fast.

**What is the best revision of this sentence?**

A   Owens went to high school. In Ohio, his classmates realized that he could run fast.

B   Owens went to Ohio to high school. Classmates realized that he could run fast.

C   Owens went to high school in Ohio, but his classmates realized that he could run fast.

D   When Owens went to high school in Ohio, his classmates realized that he could run fast.

**9**

> Jesse Owens ran for the United States. He also jumped for the United States.

**What would be the best way to combine these sentences?**

A   Jesse Owens ran, and then he jumped, for the United States.

B   Jesse Owens ran for the United States, but he also jumped.

C   He and Jesse Owens ran and jumped for the United States.

D   Jesse Owens ran and jumped for the United States.

**10**

> Earned four gold medals.

**This sentence is a fragment because —**

A   it lacks a verb

B   it is too short

C   it lacks a subject

D   it lacks variety

## Family Treasure

My family has a treasure, and we keep it in a special box. It's not gold or jewels; it's a set of diaries. They belonged to one of my ancestors, and he wrote in them every day for twenty years. His name was Thomas Sanders. He fought in the Revolutionary War. He even took his diary to war. One evening he sat on a fence and described the battlefield he had fought on earlier that day. Needless to say, it was a very sad entry. The diaries have happy moments, too. Mom says the diaries are special. The diaries show all sides of Thomas's life.

**⑪ Which of the following sentences contains unnecessary words?**

    **A** They belonged to one of my ancestors, and he wrote in them every day for twenty years.

    **B** His name was Thomas Sanders.

    **C** Needless to say, it was a very sad entry.

    **D** The diaries have happy moments, too.

**⑫ Which of the following revisions adds variety to the first three sentences of the paragraph?**

    **A** My family has a treasure, but we keep it in a special box.

    **B** We keep it in a special box, and it's not gold or jewels.

    **C** It's not gold or jewels. It's a set of diaries.

    **D** My ancestor wrote in them every day for twenty years.

**⑬**

> His name was Thomas Sanders. He fought in the Revolutionary War.

**Which is the best way to combine these sentences?**

    **A** His name was Thomas Sanders, he fought in the Revolutionary War.

    **B** Fighting in the Revolutionary War, his name was Thomas Sanders.

    **C** His name was Thomas Sanders, and he fought in the Revolutionary War.

    **D** Thomas Sanders was his name, but he fought in the Revolutionary War.

**⑭**

> One evening he sat on a fence and described the battlefield he had fought on earlier that day.

**This sentence adds variety to the paragraph because it —**

    **A** is followed by short sentences

    **B** is a simple sentence

    **C** begins the same way as the sentence before it

    **D** is preceded by a long, complex sentence

**⑮**

> Mom says the diaries are special. The diaries show all sides of Thomas's life.

**What is the best way to combine these sentences?**

    **A** Mom says the diaries are special, but they show all sides of Thomas's life.

    **B** Mom says the diaries are special because they show all sides of Thomas's life.

    **C** Mom says the diaries, while they show all sides of Thomas's life, are special.

    **D** Mom says the diaries are special, and they show all sides of Thomas's life.

## Mighty Mountains

People often think of mountains as great piles of rock. Stand tall and have no effect on humans. Mountains however, have controlled climate. Mountains have influenced travel. Mountains change climate by blocking winds. They collect moisture on one side. They prevent it from reaching the other side. Mountains serve as barriers, too. Sometimes these barriers determined where people could settle other times, they served as places of defense in wars. Many people don't understand mountains. Mountains have affected human history.

 Stand tall and have no effect on humans.

**What would be the best way to revise this sentence fragment?**

A Add a verb.

B Add a subject and a verb.

C Add a subject.

D *It does not need to be revised.*

 Mountains, however, have controlled climate. Mountains have influenced travel.

**What would be the best way to combine these two sentences?**

A Mountains, however, have controlled climate, but influenced travel.

B Mountains, however, have controlled climate and influenced travel.

C Mountains, however, have controlled climate they have influenced travel.

D Mountains have controlled climate, however, they have influenced travel.

 They collect moisture on one side. They prevent it from reaching the other side.

**What would be the best way to combine these two sentences?**

A They collect moisture on one side and prevent it from reaching the other side.

B They collect moisture on one side; also they prevent it from reaching the other side.

C When they collect moisture on one side, they, however, prevent it from reaching the other side.

D They collect and prevent moisture.

 Sometimes these barriers determined where people could settle other times, they served as places of defense in wars.

**This sentence is an example of a—**

A wordy sentence

B stringy sentence

C sentence fragment

D run-on sentence

 Many people don't understand mountains. Mountains have affected human history.

**What is the best way to combine these sentences?**

A Many people don't understand mountains, which have affected human history.

B Many people, who don't understand mountains, have affected human history.

C Many people, which don't understand mountains, have affected human history.

D Many people, who have affected human history, don't understand mountains.

# Learning About Paragraphs

**DIRECTIONS** Read each passage. Then read the questions that follow each passage. Decide which is the correct answer. Mark the space for the answer you have chosen.

---

### Paragraph 1

More than fifty exotic birds have been rescued as smugglers tried to sell them. The birds, macaws and toucans, were seized in a village in Panama. A local conservationist then took responsibility for the birds. Because they had been deprived of their native diets, however, they began to sicken and die. Fortunately, the conservationist called a veterinarian from Florida. After sending two people to help, she went to Panama herself, and they nursed the birds back to health. A proper diet consists of fresh tropical fruits and beans, along with corn, rice, and seeds. Eventually, most of the birds were released.

---

**❶ Which of the following sentences *best* states the main idea of this paragraph?**

A   More than fifty exotic birds have been rescued from smugglers.

B   The rescued birds were toucans and macaws, and they were not healthy.

C   A local conservationist, with help from a veterinarian, nursed some smuggled birds back to health.

D   Some rescued birds were deprived of their native diets and became ill.

**❷ What kinds of supporting details does this paragraph have?**

F   Statistics

G   Examples

H   Sensory details

J   Facts

**❸ Which sentence destroys the unity of the paragraph and should be removed?**

A   The birds, macaws and toucans, were seized in a village in Panama.

B   A local conservationist then took responsibility for the birds.

C   Because they had been deprived of their native diets, however, they began to sicken and die.

D   A proper diet consists of fresh tropical fruits and beans, along with corn, rice, and seeds.

**❹ How are the details in this paragraph arranged?**

F   In logical order

G   In spatial order

H   In chronological order

J   In transitional order

---

### Paragraph 2

Dear Stephanos Family Members,

Planning our family reunion has been quite a job. It has also been one of the most rewarding things I've ever done. Here are some reminders as the date approaches. First, please confirm your reservations at the hotel by May 15. Second, put a deposit on your rooms so the hotel will hold them even if you arrive late in the evening. Finally, if you want to book a tour of Charleston, let me know by June 22. I'll make the arrangements.

Sincerely,

Terry

---

**5** **Which word indicates how the details are arranged?**

A   *First*

B   *Planning*

C   *rewarding*

D   *confirm*

**6** **What transitional word does the writer use to connect two ideas?**

F   *also*, in the second sentence

G   *one*, in the second sentence

H   *some*, in the third sentence

J   *even*, in the fifth sentence

**7** **The letter would be clearer if it were divided into two paragraphs. With which sentence should the second paragraph begin?**

A   "It has also been . . ."

B   "Here are some reminders . . ."

C   "Second, put a deposit . . ."

D   "Finally, if you want to . . ."

**8** **Why does the writer arrange the details in chronological order?**

F   To explain how the readers should prepare for the reunion

G   To show the cause-and-effect chain that will occur before the reunion

H   To share information according to its location

J   To tell the story of how the writer organized the reunion

**9** **What type of paragraph is this?**

A   Narrative

B   Persuasive

C   Descriptive

D   Expository

---

## Paragraph 3

As visitors approach the Ancient Mysteries exhibit, they see a cave-like entrance. Roughly shaped stones arch gracefully to form a doorway. Through the doorway is a tunnel lit only by lanterns. The dim tunnel opens out into a bright, sandy expanse. At the left is a tent, a camp stove, and a table full of artifacts. This is a scientist's camp. Straight ahead is a stone building, perhaps a temple. To the right is the stone foundation of another structure. Some of the stones have markings on them that look like letters. Visitors are urged to explore the foundation and the stone buildings as well as the artifacts to find clues about what the buildings might have been and about the people who built them.

---

**10** The paragraph lacks a topic sentence. Which of the following is the *best* topic sentence for this paragraph?

   F   An ancient temple has been re-created at the science museum.

   G   A new museum exhibit shows us how we learn about ancient peoples.

   H   The new exhibit at the science museum came in under budget and on schedule.

   J   Museum staff are excited about the Ancient Mysteries exhibit.

**11** In what order are the details in this paragraph arranged?

   A   In chronological order

   B   In spatial order

   C   In comparison order

   D   In logical order

**12** What would be the *best* clincher sentence for this paragraph?

   F   Anyone who likes an ancient mystery or scientific exploration will enjoy this exhibit.

   G   Go see the new exhibit on ancient caves at the science museum.

   H   The buildings were constructed in 3000 B.C. by the Mayas.

   J   Visitors may talk to the museum guides, who are dressed as scientists and hold lanterns.

**13** Which of the following sentences would *best* elaborate on this statement from the paragraph: "Straight ahead is a stone building, perhaps a temple"?

   A   The museum staff are very excited about this part of the exhibit.

   B   This was the most expensive part of the exhibit.

   C   Visitors often gasp when they see it looming in front of them.

   D   Carved into its walls are fierce animal faces.

**14** What type of paragraph is this?

   F   Persuasive

   G   Expository

   H   Narrative

   J   Descriptive

**15** What is the main idea of this paragraph?

   A   The new exhibit gives a realistic look at an ancient site.

   B   Visitors to the museum will be thrilled by the new exhibit.

   C   The hands-on nature of the new exhibit makes it very popular.

   D   People who like mysteries will like this exhibit.

---

### Paragraph 4

The appeal of smooth wood on an old chair is a mystery to some, but not to me. When I look at the worn arms of a chair, I imagine tired men and women sitting in front of a fireplace. Sometimes a chair has a burn mark on the back from being tipped into the fire. The part I like best is a front rung worn smooth. Even today, children have a habit of hooking the heels of their shoes on the rung. How many children and how many years does it take to wear down a place for each heel and rub it smooth? I imagine them sitting at a meal, heels hooked on their chairs, silent until someone spoke to them. Maybe as they worked their lessons trying not to fidget, they hooked their heels onto the rung.

---

**16** Which of the following would be the best detail to add after the second sentence?

**F** They might have been waiting for company to arrive.

**G** Their hands would have rested on those arms daily, smoothing the wood.

**H** The fireplace would have been where they sat, cooking their meals.

**J** They might have owned only one or two chairs.

**17** In the sentence that begins "The part I like best..." what would be the best transitional word or phrase to add?

**A** The part I like best, at last, is ...

**B** The part I like best, often, is ...

**C** However, the part I like best is ...

**D** As a result, the part I like best is ...

**18** Which of the following sentences does *not* belong in this paragraph?

**F** When I look at the worn arms of a chair, I imagine tired men and women sitting in front of a fireplace.

**G** Sometimes a chair has a burn mark on the back from being tipped into the fire.

**H** The part I like best is a front rung worn smooth.

**J** Maybe as they worked their lessons trying not to fidget, they hooked their heels onto the rung.

**19** The sensory detail in the phrase "to wear down a place for each heel and rub it smooth" appeals to the sense of —

**A** touch

**B** smell

**C** hearing

**D** sight

**20** Which of the following would be the *best* clincher sentence for this paragraph?

**F** Garage sales are great sources of old wooden chairs.

**G** Not all wooden chairs show such signs of use, but many do.

**H** Whatever they did, the children left a sign that the chair was well used.

**J** In any case, the children sat in front of the fireplace with their parents.

# Reading Workshop: Eyewitness Account

**DIRECTIONS** *Read the passage. Then read each question about the passage. Decide which is the best answer to the question. Fill in the bubble next to the answer you have chosen. Mark like this ◯ not like this ⊘ .*

## The Roar of the Thunderbirds

The ringing phone jarred me awake. "Hello," I answered sternly, wondering who would dare to call me so early on a Saturday morning.

"Get up, Maria. We're going to an air show today. Be ready in half an hour."

Before I could object, Raul hung up. Raul usually took me to interesting events, but an air show? At that moment, sleeping late seemed much more appealing.

Still, I got dressed and greeted Raul thirty minutes later. "I expect a good show," I warned.

As he drove to the field, he described the Thunderbirds, an elite squadron of Air Force pilots. I listened in silence, too sleepy and grumpy to be excited. When we arrived, I was surprised to see a large number of people standing at the edge of a big airfield. We found a place to stand in the growing crowd.

Six gigantic F-16 jets sat on the runway. The gleaming white bodies of the fighter planes threw off a glare in the hot sun, and I shielded my eyes with my hand. I could see a cockpit covered by what looked like hard, black plastic. Raul called it a "canopy." The wings, nose, and tail of each jet were painted with three stripes. The first was red, the next white, and the last one a blue so dark that it looked like the night sky. Over each right wing were the letters USAF.

Just then, an announcement crackled over a loudspeaker. The show was beginning. Six pilots dressed in bright red jumpsuits marched briskly onto the airfield. They climbed into the

cockpits and pulled on their helmets. A loud BOOM shook the crowd as the pilots started the jet engines. The squadron leader pulled down his canopy, and the others followed in quick, precise order. The pilots then turned to the crowd, gave a thumbs-up sign, and the six jets roared off into the distance.

The squadron turned and headed back over the airfield in a diamond formation. Streams of white smoke trailed behind them in the brilliant blue sky. The jets flew so close together they looked as though their wings were actually touching. They made another pass over us, doing flips and rolls and dives. The announcer called out the names of the maneuvers: "Five Card Loop, Wing Rock-and-Roll, Cuban Eight." Several times I found myself gasping, thinking the jets were about to crash.

Back and forth, up and down, the F-16s roared overhead. Without our noticing it, one jet peeled off from the others. Suddenly it appeared out of nowhere, roaring over our heads. The ground shook. It sounded like a bomb exploding behind us.

We screamed and then laughed in relief as the single jet joined the others.

Too soon, the show was over. The Thunderbirds landed, taxied down the runway, and parked. The crowd cheered wildly as the pilots approached, shaking hands, saluting, and signing autographs. I applauded and cheered along with everyone else.

Raul looked over at me and smiled. "Well, was this worth getting up for?"

**GO ON ➡**

NAME _____     CLASS _____     DATE _____

**❷ Why was Maria irritated with Raul in the first paragraph?**

○ He did not give her enough time to get ready.

○ He forgot to call the night before.

○ He woke her up too early.

○ He usually took her to boring places.

**❷ Which of the following best describes Maria's original attitude toward the air show?**

○ reluctant

○ enthusiastic

○ neutral

○ cheerful

**❸ Which of the following sentences uses descriptive language?**

○ Before I could object, Raul hung up.

○ Raul called it a "canopy".

○ Back and forth, up and down, the F-16s roared overhead.

○ Too soon, the show was over.

**❹ The phrase, *so dark that it looked like the night sky*, is an example of —**

○ an eyewitness account

○ a figure of speech

○ common language

○ an implied main idea

**❺ The sentence, *Six pilots dressed in bright red jumpsuits marched briskly onto the airfield*, uses —**

○ context clues

○ a figure of speech

○ main points

○ precise words

**❻ Which of the following is the implied main idea of the passage?**

○ Sleeping late is fun, but so is watching an air show.

○ The writer was surprised at how much she enjoyed the air show.

○ Air shows are loud and draw large crowds.

○ The Thunderbirds are a popular attraction, and people come a long way to see them.

**❼ Why did the crowd laugh when the jet flew in from behind them?**

○ They were glad to realize they were safe.

○ They thought the pilot had lost his way.

○ They were surprised that the other jets had forgotten the single jet.

○ The announcer had just told them a funny story.

**❽ What are the Thunderbirds trained to do?**

○ take turns flying

○ watch the crowd

○ perform precise stunts

○ create extreme noise

**❾ Which of the following words describe the jets?**

○ gleaming white bodies

○ hard, black plastic

○ wings, nose, and tail

○ streams of white smoke

**❿ What answer will the writer most likely give to Raul's question in the last paragraph?**

○ "It was pretty good."

○ "It was too scary."

○ "I'm glad I got up."

○ "I like to sleep late."

# Writing Workshop: Eyewitness Account

**DIRECTIONS** The passage that follows is an early draft of a student essay. Some parts need to be rewritten. Read the passage and select the best answers for the questions that follow. Some questions are about particular sentences and ask you to improve sentence structure and word choice. Other questions refer to parts of the essay and ask you to consider organization and development. In making your decisions, follow the conventions of standard written English. After you have chosen your answer, fill in the corresponding oval on your answer sheet.

*Dear Uncle Ted,*

*(1) Our town was holding a huge street party to celebrate the year 2000. (2) My parents decided the street party would be a great way for our family to celebrate together.*

*(3) We got to the party about 9:00 P.M. and headed to the nearest bandstand. (4) A rock-and-roll band was playing golden oldies that my parents knew and loved. (5) Music with a lot of rhythm played from huge speakers. (6) My parents joined other couples who were dancing the twist and the frug.*

*(7) After eating, we headed to Munn Park. (8) Please, puh-leeze, may I get my face painted, begged my sister. (9) While she waited in line, we watched a silly circus act. (10) Clowns chased each other with pies. (11) People on stilts dodged the clowns, and dogs pedaled doggie bicycles.*

*(12) When the band stopped for a break, we went to find something to eat. (13) As we walked down Main Street, delicious smells of cooking food drifted our way. (14) The sweet smell of the funnel cakes mixed with the sharp odor of sausage reminded me of the state fair. (15) I got a big bag of popcorn that I munched on throughout the evening.*

*(16) As it got close to midnight, we headed to Lake Mirror to watch the fireworks. (17) Lasers flashed the seconds on the side of a tall building while an announcer and the crowd joined in. (18) Four, three, two, one. Happy 2000! everyone shouted. (19) The huge crowd screamed and clapped, but they were quickly drowned out by the*

*loud fireworks. (20) One after another, many fireworks zoomed into the sky. (21) They looked like exploding crayons, spreading their dazzling colors high above us.*

*(22) After the fireworks, we headed back to the parking lot, tired but happy.*

*Sincerely,*

*Martin*

1.  Which of the following sentences, if added before sentence 1, would grab the attention of the reader?
    (A) Ringing out the old and ringing in the new is part of any New Year's Eve party. I went to one in 2000 with my family.
    (B) Planning a party for New Year's Eve takes time, organization, and energy. My town and parents did the work for the year 2000.
    (C) You can find party hats, confetti, horns, and fireworks at many New Year's Eve celebrations. I saw plenty of them one year.
    (D) Three zeros certainly got my parents' attention. I'm not talking about my grades, but the year 2000.

**GO ON**

2. Which of the following represents the best revision of sentence 5?

(A) Huge speakers carried music to the crowd, and they could hear the loud beat.

(B) Music with a pulsating beat boomed from huge speakers.

(C) Loud music came from big speakers, making a noisy rhythm.

(D) Music was transmitted by huge speakers with a heavy rhythm.

3. Which of the following represents the best revision of sentence 8?

(A) "Please, puh-leeze, may I get my face painted, begged my sister?"

(B) My sister begged and begged to get her face painted.

(C) "Please, puh-leeze, may I get my face painted?" begged my sister.

(D) My sister was begging please, puh-leeze, may I get my face painted."

4. Which of the following represents the best revision of sentence 11?

(A) Performers on stilts dodged the clowns, and tiny, white poodles pedaled doggie bicycles.

(B) Performers walked around the clowns on stilts, and dogs rode little bicycles made just for them.

(C) Stilt performers dodged the clowns, and little dogs pedaled bicycles made for dogs to ride.

(D) Tiny little dogs rode around on tiny little bicycles, and people who were up on tall stilts walked around the clowns.

5. Which of the following represents the best revision of sentence 15?

(A) I got a big bag of popcorn that I ate.

(B) I got a big bag of steamy, salty popcorn that I munched on throughout the evening.

(C) I got a big bag of something to chew on throughout the evening.

(D) I got a bag of food to munch on throughout the evening.

6. Which of the following represents the best revision of sentence 18?

(A) Everyone shouted, Four, three, two one. Happy 2000!

(B) "Four, three, two, one. Happy 2000! everyone shouted."

(C) "Four, three, two, one. Happy 2000!" everyone shouted.

(D) "Four, three, two, one. Happy 2000, everyone shouted!"

7. Which of the following represents the best revision of sentence 19?

(A) The huge crowd was noisy, but the loud fireworks were even noiser than the crowd's clapping and screaming.

(B) The huge crowd screamed and clapped, but it was quickly drowned out by the booming fireworks.

(C) The crowd screamed, clapped, and made lots of noise, but that was quickly drowned out by the loud fireworks.

(D) The huge crowd made lots and lots of noise by celebrating, but they were quickly drowned out by the loud fireworks.

**GO ON** ➡

8. Which of the following represents the best revision of sentence 20?

   (A) One after another, pretty fireworks zoomed into the sky.

   (B) One after another, lots of fireworks zoomed into the sky.

   (C) One after another, large fireworks zoomed into the sky.

   (D) One after another, brilliant fireworks zoomed into the sky.

9. Which of the following changes would help the organization of the passage?

   (A) Switch paragraphs 2 and 3.

   (B) Switch paragraphs 3 and 4.

   (C) Switch paragraphs 4 and 5.

   (D) Switch paragraphs 2 and 4.

10. Which sentence, if added after sentence 22, would represent the best way to conclude the letter?

   (A) I will never forget the night we welcomed the year 2000.

   (B) I think all towns should sponsor street parties for New Year's Eve.

   (C) I suggested that we stop at a restaurant on the way home.

   (D) I will wear more comfortable shoes at the next street party.

# Reading Workshop: Instructions

## Paddling a Canoe

**DIRECTIONS** *Paddling a canoe can be fun and challenging. Read the following passage to learn more about the art of canoe paddling.*

They glide silently through the water, barely creating a ripple. With the help of a river current, they use very little energy. What are they? Canoes, of course. Canoes can be great fun because it is simple to learn to paddle them.

Before you learn to canoe, you need to be able to identify the parts of the canoe. The front of a canoe is called the bow, and the back is called the stern. You can tell the front from the back by looking at the seats. The seat with the most legroom between it and the tip of the canoe is in the bow.

You also need to know basic safety precautions. Always make sure both you and your partner have a life jacket or personal flotation device (PFD). Wear some kind of footgear. Even an old pair of sneakers will give you traction when getting into and out of the canoe. An overwhelming number of paddling injuries are the result of canoeing in bare feet. You must choose a body of water that is beginner-friendly. A shallow lake or pond is ideal.

The first step is to learn to get into and out of the canoe without capsizing it. About 90 percent of all canoeing accidents occur as people are trying to get into the canoe. In order to board a canoe safely, first push the canoe into the water, keeping the craft parallel to the shore. While holding on to the top sides of the canoe, step quickly into the center and kneel. Stay in a low position and move to the bow or the stern. Your partner should then follow the same procedure.

Next, practice holding your paddle correctly. If you are paddling on the right side, hold your right hand on the shaft of the paddle, near the top of the blade. Place your left hand on the paddle's grip. Your hands should be about a shoulder width apart, and your arms should remain straight most of the time you are paddling. Your partner should paddle on the opposite side of the canoe.

Now begin to move the paddle. The basic stroke for the person in the bow is the forward stroke. Reach out as far as you can over the water with your paddle without straining. Keep your top hand about shoulder height. Place the blade of the paddle in the water and pull it straight back, keeping the paddle parallel to the canoe. When the paddle reaches your hips, swivel the blade out of the water. Repeat the stroke to move forward. To make a left turn, reach forward on the right side with the paddle, place it in the water, and trace a C in the water with a sweeping motion.

If the canoe starts to go off course, you or your partner in the stern must use the J stroke to correct it. Reaching forward, place the paddle in the water and pull back. At the end of the stroke, twist the paddle outward, in the form of a J. You must use the J stroke for every third or fourth stroke to keep the canoe on course.

Learn these strokes and you are well on your way to enjoying the adventure of canoeing.

**GO ON →**

1. What is the author's overall purpose for writing this passage?

   A  to show how to place a canoe in the water

   B  to prepare readers for white-water canoeing

   C  to tell readers the basic steps in canoeing

   D  to stress the importance of life preservers

2. What is the author's purpose in paragraph 1?

   A  to interest readers in the activity

   B  to describe canoes

   C  to convince someone to go to the river

   D  to tell a personal experience with a canoe

3. What should you learn first?

   A  the parts of the canoe

   B  how to put on a life preserver

   C  how to hold the paddle

   D  how to get into the canoe safely

4. What is the author's purpose in paragraph 3?

   A  to warn the reader about accidents

   B  to give examples of poor safety practices

   C  to show the humor of wearing shoes

   D  to list several safety precautions

5. After putting the canoe in the water, what is the next step in getting into a canoe?

   A  move quickly to the bow or the stern

   B  push the canoe off shore with the paddle

   C  hand the shaft of your paddle to your partner

   D  hold the sides and step into the center

6. What is the author's purpose for writing the paragraph about getting into the canoe?

   A  to help beginning canoeists avoid accidents

   B  to teach inexperienced canoeists how to paddle

   C  to show the importance of having a partner

   D  to help beginning canoeists avoid damaging the canoe

7. What should you learn right after learning how to get into the canoe?

   A  the parts of the paddle

   B  how to hold the canoe

   C  how to hold the paddle

   D  the C and J strokes

8. What is the first step in the forward stroke?

   A  putting the blade in the water

   B  pulling the paddle straight back

   C  turning the paddle up and out

   D  reaching far out with the paddle

9. What is the author's purpose in writing the next-to-last paragraph?

   A  to show that canoeing takes skill and practice

   B  to show how to keep the canoe on course

   C  to show the difference between strokes

   D  to show how to turn the canoe left

10. What is the last step in performing a C stroke?

   A  tracing a C in the water

   B  reaching forward with the paddle

   C  placing the paddle in the water

   D  swiveling the blade of the paddle

# Writing Workshop: Instructions

**DIRECTIONS** The passage that follows is an early draft of a student essay. Use it to answer questions 1–10.

## Making a Sports Scrapbook

Your soccer team has just won the big tournament on a kick-off. Although your memories of the event are vivid now, those memories may fade quickly.

To make a scrapbook, gather supplies. You will need a scrapbook, scissors, a photo-mounting glue stick, and colored paper. You can also buy stickers, fancy paper, and scissors, like pinking shears, that cut decorative edges.

Next, line up the items you want to put in the scrapbook. Be sure to collect candid pictures, team photos, tickets, game programs, ribbons, and newspaper articles. It is too bad that your trophies will not fit in a scrapbook. Then, arrange the items in chronological order. A team photo, for example, would probably go near the beginning of the scrapbook. Near the end of the scrapbook you would put pictures or write-ups of the tournament.

The next step is to try out different layouts of the pages before you glue things down. Place pictures and items loosely on the page to get a general idea of what will fit. Begin cropping, or trimming, pictures to remove unnecessary background or to make interesting shapes.

Next, add color and visual interest by framing pictures with colored paper. This is called matting. Simply glue the picture onto a piece of colored paper, and then cut the paper to the size you want. One time I glued a picture to the wrong paper, and I had a terrible time getting it unstuck. Make sure the pictures will still fit on the page.

With your final layout in mind, put your pictures and items into your scrapbook. Before applying glue, think about and leave room for headlines, captions, and journal entries. Headlines and captions help to identify people, dates, and places that you might forget later.

When you have finished writing your headlines, captions, and text, your scrapbook is done! Congratulations!

**GO ON** ➡

**2** **Which sentence should be added to the introductory paragraph?**

A  It is easy to forget names, dates, and places after a year.

B  After all, sports is a very important part of many teenagers' lives.

C  One way to preserve your memories is to create a sports scrapbook.

D  Many people enjoy looking at a scrapbook and enjoying memories of good times.

**2**

> To make a scrapbook, gather supplies.

**How is this sentence best written?**

A  In making a scrapbook, the first step is to gather supplies.

B  Then, to make a scrapbook, gather all the supplies you need.

C  The next step in making a scrapbook is to gather supplies.

D  *As it is*

**3** **Which sentence would be best added as an explanation at the end of the second paragraph?**

A  Making a scrapbook sometimes can be very expensive.

B  Most craft and discount stores carry scrapbook materials.

C  I try to borrow scrapbook supplies from my mother.

D  Scrapbooks come in many different sizes and colors.

**4** **Which sentence does not belong in the third paragraph?**

A  Be sure to collect candid pictures, team photos, tickets, game programs, ribbons, and newspaper articles.

B  It is too bad that your trophies will not fit in a scrapbook.

C  Then, arrange the items in chronological order.

D  A team photo, for example, would probably go near the beginning of the scrapbook.

**5** **How should <u>Near the end of the scrapbook</u> be written?**

A  Near the end of the scrapbook,

B  Near the end, of the scrapbook

C  Near the end of the scrapbook;

D  *As it is*

**6**

> Begin cropping, or trimming, pictures to remove unnecessary background or to make interesting shapes.

**What sentence would be best added after this sentence?**

A  Scissors make the cropping job simple, but be sure to use them carefully.

B  Just be sure that you do not try to put so many pictures on a page that it looks crowded.

C  Most people don't take very good pictures because they shoot them from too far away.

D  For example, the shape of a football goes along with memories of a football game.

Which of the following sentences does not belong in paragraph 5?

**A** Next, add color and visual interest by framing pictures with colored paper.

**B** Simply glue the picture onto a piece of colored paper, and then cut the paper to the size you want.

**C** One time I glued a picture to the wrong paper, and I had a terrible time getting it unstuck.

**D** This is called matting.

**8**

> Make sure the pictures will still fit on the page.

**How is this sentence best written?**

**A** Making sure they will still fit on the page is also part of this process.

**B** Don't forget to make sure they will still fit on the page that you are working on.

**C** After matting the pictures, make sure they will still fit on the scrapbook page.

**D** *As it is*

> With your final layout in mind, put your pictures and items into your scrapbook.

**To keep this step in order, this sentence should —**

**A** be deleted from the paragraph

**B** be put in the next paragraph

**C** come at the end of the paragraph

**D** remain where it is

> Congratulations!

**Which of the following should be added after this sentence as a conclusion for the essay?**

**A** Making a scrapbook takes time, hard work, and money, but it is a fun hobby.

**B** Now that you have made your first scrapbook, you can join a scrapbook club to improve your skills.

**C** Any job worth doing, is worth doing well, and your scrapbook is no exception.

**D** Your winning sports season and all its exciting memories are now preserved for years to come.

# Reading Workshop: Advantages/Disadvantages Article

**DIRECTIONS** *A student has written this report for English class. She explores the advantages and disadvantages of physical education, or P.E. When you finish reading the report, answer the multiple choice questions that follow.*

## The Good, the Bad, and the Ugly

Remember the days when you counted the minutes until recess? Remember when a rousing game of kickball during physical education class made your pulse pound from excitement? Remember when you considered the ball field and the court to be the most hallowed ground in school?

2 That was then, you may say. Now that you are out of elementary school, you would probably say that you are over P.E. Well, you are not alone. Most middle and high schoolers avoid P.E. Some absolutely hate the thought of gym class. Let's face it: P.E. has plenty of negatives. Lack of privacy in locker rooms is a big drawback. In elementary school, no one had to change clothes for P.E. and take showers. Then there is the hair issue to consider. The term *bad hair day* was probably coined by a student looking in the mirror after gym class.

3 Another liability for some students is lack of athletic ability. It's embarrassing to strike out, throw air balls, or come in last, especially in front of your peers. Some kids may have a little talent but simply lack interest in sports. They would rather be playing an instrument or working on the computer than doing something physical. Why must they participate in something that they do not enjoy?

4 For all its drawbacks, however, P.E. has some very definite benefits. The most obvious benefit is that it provides the opportunity for regular exercise. Most teens—about 62 percent—do not

get enough exercise. P.E. at least offers students a chance to move their bodies.

5 Consider other benefits of regular exercise in P.E. A huge advantage for appearance-conscious teens is weight control. Everyone knows that exercise burns calories. Regular exercise, along with a healthful diet, helps keep weight off. If you want to lose weight to look better, P.E. can help you. Or are you too stressed to think about P.E.? Exercise can help with that, too. Studies show that people feel less anxious and more relaxed after exercising. School or friends might be stressing you out, but exercise may be one possible solution to your problems.

6 Then there are all the long-lasting health advantages of exercise. If you exercise, you are less likely to be obese as an adult. Overweight teens generally grow into overweight adults. Obese adults are at risk for developing all kinds of serious medical problems, such as diabetes, heart disease, high blood pressure, cancer, and arthritis. Besides making you look and feel better, P.E. could literally save your life.

7 Many schools now make P.E. an elective instead of a requirement. Considering its drawbacks, you may be tempted to skip it altogether. When you are worrying about what P.E. may do to your hair, however, consider what it does for the rest of your body. When you think about it, a few bad hair days might not seem so bad after all.

**GO ON** ▶

1  Reading the questions in Paragraph 1 would lead you to conclude that the writer is describing —
   A  summertime
   B  elementary school
   C  camp
   D  high school

2  From reading Paragraph 2, you could conclude that —
   F  teenagers are self-conscious
   G  most teenagers like getting dressed in front of each other
   H  P.E. teachers are some of the least popular teachers
   J  teenagers prefer to take P.E. early in the day

3  Which of the following sentences in Paragraph 2 provides a clue word for advantages and disadvantages?
   A  "That was then, you may say."
   B  "Well, you are not alone."
   C  "Lack of privacy in locker rooms is a big drawback."
   D  "Then there is the hair issue to consider."

4  From reading the last sentences in Paragraph 2, you can conclude that —
   F  students do not carry combs to P.E.
   G  P.E. teachers don't care how students look
   H  locker rooms don't have enough mirrors
   J  P.E. sometimes messes up a student's hair

5  In Paragraph 3, the writer lists striking out to show that —
   A  most middle and high schoolers are not good athletes
   B  students think being embarrassed is a disadvantage of P. E.
   C  kids are more interested in computers than P.E.
   D  teens believe that making mistakes is a benefit of P.E.

6  The writer has structured the essay so that —
   F  the advantages of the topic are discussed first
   G  the disadvantages of the topic are discussed first
   H  advantages and disadvantages are discussed in the same paragraphs
   J  the reader cannot easily identify the disadvantages

7  Which of the following is used as a clue word for advantages and disadvantages in Paragraph 3?
   A  "especially"
   B  "embarrassing"
   C  "physical"
   D  "liability"

8  A logical conclusion to make from reading Paragraph 4 is that —
   F  most teens need the exercise P.E. offers
   G  P.E. cannot take the place of sports
   H  most teens participate in an exercise program
   J  P.E. is not as beneficial as exercising after school

9  Paragraph 5 supports the idea that —
   A  an advantage to taking P.E. is watching your friends
   B  most teenagers will be more stressed if they have P.E.
   C  a disadvantage to P.E. is that teenagers are concerned about their looks
   D  teens can benefit from the regular exercise in P.E.

10  From reading the essay's conclusion, you can tell that —
   F  many schools will change their policies about P.E.
   G  taking P.E. will become more popular with teens
   H  the writer believes that P.E. should be an elective
   J  the writer believes that students should take P.E.

# Writing Workshop: Advantages/ Disadvantages Essay

**DIRECTIONS** *The following essay was written by a student for English class. Read the passage (which may contain some errors) and answer the questions that follow. Be sure to fill in the bubble next to the answer you choose. Mark like this ◯ not like this ⌐⊘ . You may look back at the passage as you answer the questions.*

## The Summer Dilemma

1  Ahhh … the lazy days of summer. Sleeping late, hanging out with friends, and

2  swimming make summer one of my favorite times of the year. Last year, how-

3  ever, I discovered another reason to love summer: camp. Maybe you are con-

4  sidering making camp part of your summer.

5  Although I enjoyed my experience, camp is not for everyone. There are some

6  definite disadvantages. In my opinion, however, the disadvantages are very

7  minor ones. The first and most obvious is that you are away from home. You

8  are away from familiar people, places, and foods, and you might get homesick.

9  Trying different foods at camp is one advantage. There is very little choice at

10  meals if you don't like what is being served, you go hungry. Last, you have to

11  be willing to make new friends. Your group of friends from home will not be at

12  camp. It can be scary to go to a place where no one knows you.

13  Camp has incredible advantages that definitely outweigh the tiny disadvan-

14  tages. One of the biggest benefits of camp is trying new activities. For example,

15  I went horseback riding for the very first time at camp. One drawback to riding

16  horses is you have to clean the stalls. I also went sailing, and I tried rock climb-

17  ing, but I would not have participated in these activities at home. Another

18  benefit of camp is making friends with many people. I made friends with a girl

19  named Tasha, who is very smart. We hit it off so well! That experience has

20  helped me break out of my clique, now I try to make new friends at home.

21  Going to summer camp means taking risks. If you are up for a risk, think about

22  camp.

**2** **Which sentence, if added to the end of the first paragraph, would serve as part of a main idea statement?**

○ Summer camp has some big advantages that no one had discussed with me.

○ Knowing what to expect is a big part of being ready to go to camp for the first time.

○ If you are informed, you can talk more knowledgeably about camp to your parents.

○ If so, you want to think carefully about both its advantages and disadvantages.

**2** **Which sentence does not belong in the second paragraph?**

○ Trying different foods at camp is one advantage. (line 9)

○ The first and most obvious is that you are away from home. (line 7)

○ Last, you have to be willing to make new friends. (lines 10–11)

○ There are some definite disadvantages. (lines 5–6)

**3** **Which of the following is preferable to the sentence beginning, *There is very little choice . . .* in lines 9–10?**

○ There is very little choice at meals you might not like what is being served so you go hungry.

○ With little choice at meals; you might go hungry.

○ The food is really terrible, so if you don't like it, you go hungry.

○ There is very little choice at meals; if you don't like what is being served, you go hungry.

**4** **Which of the following sentences, if inserted, would provide the best support for the sentence beginning, *You are away from familiar people . . .* in lines 7–8?**

○ My parents sent me letters and care packages, so I did not feel very homesick.

○ My counselor said that at least one camper each season leaves camp because of homesickness.

○ I was not very worried about being homesick because I like new people, places, and foods.

○ My little sister can't even spend the night at a friend's house without getting homesick.

**5** **Which of the following does not belong in the third paragraph?**

○ One of the biggest benefits of camp is trying new activities. (line 14)

○ We hit it off so well! (line 19)

○ One drawback to riding horses is you have to clean the stalls. (lines 15–16)

○ Another benefit of camp is making friends with many people. (lines 17–18)

**GO ON** ➡

**6** **Which of the following is preferable to the sentence beginning, *I also went sailing . . .* in lines 16–17?**

○ I also went sailing. I also went rock climbing. I would not have participated in these activities at home.

○ I also went sailing, I climbed a rock, I would not have participated in these activities at home.

○ I also went sailing, which I would not have done at home, and I also went rock climbing, which I also would not have done at home.

○ I also went sailing and tried rock climbing. I would not have participated in these activities at home.

**7** **Which of the following sentences shows bias and should be revised?**

○ It can be scary to go to a place where no one knows you. (line 12)

○ Camp has incredible advantages that definitely outweigh the tiny disadvantages. (lines 13–14)

○ Going to summer camp means taking risks. (line 21)

○ Maybe you are considering making camp part of your summer. (lines 3–4)

**8** **Which of the following sentences needs a semicolon to keep it from being a run-on sentence?**

○ If you are up for a risk, think about camp. (lines 21–22)

○ Last year, however, I discovered another reason to love summer: camp. (lines 2–3)

○ That experience has helped me break out of my clique, now I try to make new friends at home. (lines 19–20)

○ I made friends with a girl named Tasha, who is very smart. (lines 18–19)

**9** **Which of the following sentences shows bias and needs to be revised?**

○ In my opinion, however, the disadvantages are very minor ones. (lines 6–7)

○ Although I enjoyed my experience, camp is not for everyone. (line 5)

○ Your group of friends from home will not be at camp. (lines 11–12)

○ One of the biggest benefits of camp is trying new activities. (line 14)

**10** **Which sentence, if added after the first sentence of the last paragraph, would improve the essay's conclusion? (line 21)**

○ The risks of having to make new friends, eat new foods, and deal with homesickness might scare you off.

○ Sometimes people do not like to take risks at summer camp.

○ Of course, it is best not to think of the disadvantages.

○ Of course, the risk of being homesick exists, but camp provides the opportunity for many new experiences.

# Reading Workshop: Novel's Book Jacket

**DIRECTIONS** Read the book jacket for the novel *The Yearling* before answering Numbers 1 through 10 on the Answer Sheet.

### Front Cover

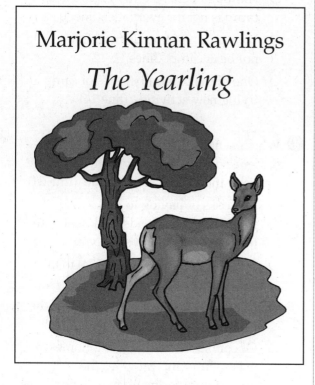

Marjorie Kinnan Rawlings
*The Yearling*

### Back Cover

He was prepared for trouble. He was prepared for something ominous that had dogged him for days. He was not prepared for the impossible. He was not prepared for his father's words.

### Front Flap

Adventure, hard work, and wonder fill the days of twelve-year-old Jody Baxter, who lives in Florida's wild scrub country. His family, facing constant threats from bears, wolves, snakes, and other predators, lives by the code, "Eat or be eaten. Kill or go hungry." The scrub country, however, also offers Jody the pleasures of rambling through the pine woods, fishing at the sinkhole, and watching whooping cranes perform a magical dance.

As an only child, Jody longs for the companionship of a pet. His wish is answered when a rattlesnake bites his father, and he kills a doe to use its heart and liver to draw out the snake's poison. The doe leaves behind an orphaned fawn, which Jody quickly adopts as a pet and names Flag. The fawn becomes Jody's constant companion.

The book traces the transformation of Jody from a boy to a man and Flag from a fawn to a yearling. Hardships through the winter, however, threaten the very survival of the Baxter family. When Flag eats some corn shoots, Jody's mother loses her patience. Jody faces a heart-wrenching decision. Will he become the man his family needs him to be, or will he reject their needs in favor of his own?

### Back Flap

Marjorie Kinnan Rawlings moved to Cross Creek, Florida, in 1928 at the age of thirty-two. She immediately fell in love with Florida's scrub country and its people.

Making sure her books were true to life was important to Rawlings. For her novel *South Moon Under*, Rawlings lived with a family in the Florida scrub for ten weeks. Later, while outlining *The Yearling*, she contacted a guide and joined him on several bear hunts.

*The Yearling*, Rawlings's third novel about Florida's scrub country, was published in 1938. Reviewers hailed it as a masterpiece. It quickly became a bestseller and then won the Pultizer Prize for fiction in 1939. A movie version of the book was released in 1946 and received several Oscar nominations, including one for Best Picture.

**GO ON** ➡

❷ You can tell from looking at the front cover that

   **A.**  the story will appeal to sports fans.

   **B.**  the story is set in a city zoo.

   **C.**  one of the main characters is a deer.

   **D.**  deer are not safe from hunters.

❷ Which of the following is a logical question to ask after looking at the book's front cover?

   **F.**  What will happen to the fawn?

   **G.**  Why did hunters kill the fawn's mother?

   **H.**  What crops do the Baxters plant?

   **I.**  When did the author write the book?

❸ The book's title and the cover picture might lead you to conclude that

   **A.**  *yearling* is a nickname for Jody.

   **B.**  *yearling* refers to the gender of the deer.

   **C.**  *yearling* is a term for a young animal.

   **D.**  *yearling* refers to a full-grown animal.

❹ After previewing the novel, you could logically predict that

   **F.**  the Baxters will move out of the scrub and into town.

   **G.**  Jody will experience both joy and pain because of Flag.

   **H.**  Flag will save Jody's father by rescuing him from a bear.

   **I.**  Jody's family will raise more forest animals.

❺ Based on the excerpt on the back cover, what could you logically predict will happen in the book?

   **A.**  Jody will face a terrible situation concerning Flag.

   **B.**  Jody's father will follow Flag and Jody through the woods.

   **C.**  Jody will get tired of all the work involved in taking care of Flag.

   **D.**  Jody will never learn to take responsibility for his actions.

❻ Based on the information given on the front flap, you could logically describe Jody as

   **F.**  irresponsible.

   **G.**  sensitive.

   **H.**  rebellious.

   **I.**  scared.

❼ Based on the front flap, what could you predict will most likely happen in the book?

   **A.**  Jody's father will not recover from the rattlesnake bite.

   **B.**  Jody's mother will build a fence around the corn.

   **C.**  Jody will hide Flag from his family.

   **D.**  Jody will struggle to make a decision.

❽ Which question could you BEST use to create a purpose as you read *The Yearling*?

   **F.**  How long does it take to die from a rattlesnake bite?

   **G.**  Why did Rawlings move to Florida?

   **H.**  How does Jody choose a name for the fawn?

   **I.**  What problems does Jody have because he keeps the fawn?

❾ From the back flap, you might conclude that

   **A.**  the description of Cross Creek will be unrealistic.

   **B.**  the movie version of *The Yearling* is no longer popular.

   **C.**  the author develops themes that appeal to many readers.

   **D.**  many people will not recognize the title of the book.

❿ After previewing *The Yearling*, you would probably recommend it to people who

   **F.**  want to learn about hunting.

   **G.**  need information about history.

   **H.**  love realistic stories about animals.

   **I.**  enjoy lighthearted books.

# Writing Workshop: Jacket for a Novel

**DIRECTIONS** Antonia created this rough draft of her book jacket. Use it to answer questions 1–10.

**Front Cover**

Robert Louis Stevenson
**Treasure Island**

HISPANIOLA

## Back Cover

It was a bright enough little place of entertainment. The sign was newly painted; the windows had neat red curtains; the floor was cleanly sanded.

## Front Flap

A dead pirate's map to buried treasure leads young Jim Hawkins on a wild adventure. Two family friends, Dr. Livesey and Squire Trelawney, hire a ship and crew to take the three of them to the treasure.

Once the *Hispaniola* sets sail, however, Jim discovers the terrifying truth. Many of the sailors they have hired are pirates, and Silver is their leader! The pirates plan to take the treasure and the ship. The pirates plot to kill Jim and the others.

Treachery, mutiny, deception, and adventure mark the rest of the voyage as Jim matches wits with the sly Silver. Can he survive the voyage and beat the others to the treasure? Can these ruthless pirates be overcome? After a long struggle, the three are able to find the treasure, overcome the pirates, and return home safely with their riches.

Readers will recognize and enjoy the timeless battle between good and evil in this fast-moving and thrilling adventure story.

## Back Flap

Robert Louis Stevenson wrote *Treasure Island* in his early thirties. By then he was already a well-known writer. The ideas for the story came from tales he had heard, people he had known, and stories he had read.

*Treasure Island* first appeared as a serial story in a boys' magazine. It was <u>published</u> in book form in 1883. Through the years, critics have praised it for its wonderful characterization, fast-moving plot, descriptions, and realistic dialogue.

**GO ON** ➡

**❷ The image of the *Hispaniola* on the front cover —**

   A  does a good job of capturing the reader's interest

   B  needs to be replaced with a more meaningful image

   C  gives away too much of the story and should be replaced

   D  accurately reflects the content of the book

**❷ Which sentence serves as the hook on the front flap?**

   A  Two family friends, Dr. Livesey and Squire Trelawney, hire a ship and crew to take the three of them to the treasure.

   B  Can these ruthless pirates be overcome?

   C  A dead pirate's map to buried treasure leads young Jim Hawkins on a wild adventure.

   D  Readers will recognize and enjoy the timeless battle between good and evil in this fast-moving and thrilling adventure story.

**❸ Which of the following elements is described least in the summary on the front flap?**

   A  characters

   B  plot

   C  theme

   D  setting

**❹ Which of these sentences about the novel's characters should be included at the beginning of paragraph 2 on the front flap?**

   A  The ship's cook is Long John Silver, a cheerful, friendly, one-legged sailor who quickly gains the confidence of Jim and his companions.

   B  Jim's mother and father run the Admiral Benbow, an inn in England, where Jim meets many unusual visitors, such as Billy Bones.

   C  Captain Smollet has on his crew a mate, a quartermaster, a coxswain named Israel Hands, a boatswain, and a gunner.

   D  Stevenson modeled the character of Long John Silver on his good friend William E. Henley.

**❺**

> The pirates plan to take the treasure and the ship. The pirates plot to kill Jim and the others.

**How are these sentences best combined without changing their meaning?**

   A  The pirates plan to take the treasure, and then plot to take the ship and to kill Jim and the others.

   B  The pirates plan to take the treasure, plotting to take the ship and killing Jim and the others.

   C  They plan to take the treasure and the ship; they plot to kill Jim and the others.

   D  The pirates plan to take the treasure and the ship, and they plot to kill Jim and the others.

**❻ How should <u>pub-lished</u> be written?**

   A  publish-ed

   B  publishe-d

   C  publi-shed

   D  *As it is*

**7** The sentences that were chosen for the back cover —

A successfully grab the reader's attention

B help the reader to understand what the story is about

C need to be replaced with a shorter passage

D need to be replaced with a more interesting passage

**8** Which sentence does *not* belong in the summary on the front flap?

A Once the *Hispaniola* sets sail, however, Jim discovers the terrifying truth.

B Can he suvive the voyage and beat the others to the treasure?

C After a long struggle, the three are able to find the treasure, overcome the pirates, and return home safely with their riches.

D A dead pirate's map to buried treasure leads young Jim Hawkins on a wild adventure.

**9** Which of the following sentences should be added after the last sentence on the front flap?

A They will also discover, as Jim does, that most people are not entirely good or totally evil.

B They will also enjoy meeting Long John Silver's parrot, Captain Flint, who is named after a famous pirate.

C *Treasure Island* was not very popular in its magazine form, but it became a big success as a book.

D The dialogue is very realistic and sometimes hard to understand, but it does not detract from the book.

**10** Which of these can best be added to paragraph 1 of the author's biography to increase the reader's interest in the book?

A His father and grandfather were both light-house engineers. Stevenson's father was not pleased when his son turned to writing as a career.

B Stevenson published a book of poetry called *A Child's Garden of Verses* in 1885. He dedicated the book to his Scottish nurse, who cared for him in childhood.

C He got the idea for *Treasure Island* when doodling with a pen and watercolors. He sketched a map of an island and knew he must write a novel.

D Stevenson and his wife lived their last years in Samoa, where he won the friendship of the local people. They are both buried on the top of Mount Vaea.

# Reading Workshop: Informative Article

**DIRECTIONS** Read the passage. Read each question and choose the best answer. Mark the space for the answer you have chosen.

## Understanding Dyslexia

Albert Einstein, whom *Time* magazine named its person of the twentieth century, was a genius. Surprisingly, he was a late talker and a poor student. During his early schooling, teachers thought he was not very smart. Einstein was dyslexic. Although dyslexia afflicts between 10 and 15 percent of the American population, most people know very little about it.

### What Is Dyslexia?

Dyslexia is a language disorder. The word *dyslexia* comes from two Greek words: *dys-*, meaning difficult, and *lexis*, meaning word. Literally translated, *dyslexia* means difficulty with words. Dyslexia may be a neurological condition, which means that it is caused by the way the brain functions. Dyslexia often runs in families, leading researchers to believe it may be an inherited condition. Researchers once thought that boys were four times as likely to have dyslexia as girls. The latest studies, however, show that girls are just as likely to be dyslexic as boys.

### Symptoms of Dyslexia

Dyslexia can range from mild to severe, and the condition is as unique as the people who have it. Signs of dyslexia include difficulty in learning how to read and spell. In cases of mild dyslexia, this symptom might not become obvious until later elementary school or even high school, when language and texts become more complex. Confusing directions, such as right and left, is another symptom of dyslexia. Many dyslexics have trouble spelling words. Many dyslexics cannot create rhymes. Reversing letters, such as writing a *b* for *d* or reading *saw* for *was*, may also be a symptom.

### How Dyslexia Affects Learning

Dyslexics have trouble understanding the relationship between letters and sounds. The English language has forty-four sounds, called **phonemes**. The word *cat*, for example, is made up of three phonemes: *kuh*, *aa*, and *tuh*. Learning to read involves identifying these phonemes, matching them to letters, and blending the sounds together to make words. Most people sound out words so quickly that the process is automatic. This decoding process, however, is rarely automatic for dyslexics. Thus, they often read at a slower rate than others.

### Misconceptions About Dyslexia

Because dyslexic children have difficulty learning to read, some people jump to the wrong conclusion that these children are not bright. As the example of Einstein shows, dyslexia is not a sign of low intelligence. Many dyslexics are highly creative and talented people. Walt Disney, Mohammed Ali, Whoopi Goldberg, Winston Churchill, and Tom Cruise are people who overcame dyslexia to succeed.

Some people mistakenly believe that dyslexics are lazy and just need to work harder. Most dyslexic students, however, work incredibly hard but require a different kind of instruction. Multisensory instruction is helpful; many dyslexics learn better by using visual aids, touch, and movement. Students may also need instruction in phonics to help them match phonemes to letters more readily.

Dyslexia can be a challenge, but it does not mean failure. Just ask any of the accomplished and successful people who have learned how to live with dyslexia.

**2** **Which of these is an example of a textbook feature used in the article?**

A  diagrams

B  reference notes

C  charts

D  headings

**2** **Which of these sentences best summarizes the definition of dyslexia in the article?**

A  Dyslexia is a condition that affected Einstein.

B  Dyslexia is a neurological condition that causes problems in processing language.

C  Dyslexia is a disease that shows up about fourth grade or later.

D  Dyslexia is a learning problem that occurs when students are not taught to read properly.

**3** **According to the article, how does dyslexia affect boys and girls?**

A  Boys and girls have dyslexia at about the same rates.

B  Four times as many boys have dyslexia as girls.

C  Girls have less severe dyslexia than boys.

D  Only boys inherit dyslexia.

**4** **The article's headings indicate that it will —**

A  define dyslexia, describe its symptoms, and discuss misconceptions

B  explain medical and educational research

C  focus on various treatments throughout history

D  explain how teachers and parents can help

**5** **Which of these sentences best explains symptoms of dyslexia?**

A  The most common symptom of dyslexia is reversing letters and numbers.

B  Dyslexia has very few symptoms, so it is almost impossible to diagnose.

C  Difficulties in reading and spelling are common symptoms.

D  Everyone has the same symptoms.

**6** **Why does the word *phoneme* appear in boldface type?**

A  to highlight its suffix

B  to break information into chunks

C  to show where to find more information

D  to point to an important concept

**7** **According to the article, how does dyslexia affect learning?**

A  Dyslexia is caused by reading words too slowly.

B  Dyslexia makes it difficult to decode the sounds of language.

C  Blending sounds is automatic for people with dyslexia.

D  Dyslexia mainly affects memory.

**8** **A study guide made from the textbook features of this article should include —**

A  important vocabulary

B  graphs

C  marginal notes

D  paragraphs

**9** **Which is the best summary of the section on misconceptions of dyslexia?**

A  Many dyslexics are highly creative people.

B  Many famous people have dyslexia.

C  Learning phonics can cure dyslexia.

D  People with dyslexia are not stupid or lazy.

**10** **If you were making a study guide for this passage, you would definitely include —**

A  a summary of the symptoms of dyslexia

B  the names of famous people with dyslexia

C  a graph showing important statistics about dyslexia

D  a list of researchers who have studied this problem

TEST
# Writing Workshop: Report of Information

**DIRECTIONS** *Kanetra has written this essay for technology class. As part of a peer writing conference, you are asked to read the report and think about what suggestions you would make. When you finish reading the report, answer the multiple-choice questions that follow.*

## Virtual Reality

1    Imagine taking a field trip to Mars or going inside the human heart. Does
2    this sound impossible? With virtual reality, you may soon be taking these
3    kinds of field trips. In fact, researchers are discovering new ways to use virtual
4    reality in medicine.

5    According to one definition, virtual reality is "a computer-created environ-
6    ment that simulates real-life situations." In other words, a computer allows a
7    viewer to see, hear, feel, and move around in a world that seems very real.
8    Teachers think students will especially enjoy using virtual reality. To experi-
9    ence virtual reality, people must wear special helmets, gloves, or glasses.

10    Virtual reality already helps many people do their jobs better. Virtual reali-
11    ty helps doctors practice surgery and other risky procedures without jeopar-
12    dizing real patients. Some experts predict that medical students will one day
13    "study anatomy by dissecting virtual bodies" instead of cadavers.

14    Police in England are experimenting with a virtual reality system to look at
15    crime scenes in a new way. Police in England asked researchers to recreate a
16    garage where a murder took place. By using special 3-D glasses, the detectives
17    were able to "fly" around the garage. They could look at the scene from differ-
18    ent angles and see what different witnesses could actually see while the crime
19    was being committed.

20    In sports, virtual reality is taking instant replay one step further. A viewer
21    can use a new program called Virtual Replay to fabricate the field and calcu-
22    late the whereabouts of the players. A viewer can enter the scene, which is
23    three dimensional, and look at the play from any angle or camera point. In the
24    past, a referee, who would not be limited to just a couple of camera angles,
25    used instant replay regularly.

26    Virtual reality was once used only for entertainment.

27 ## Works Cited

28    Grumet, Tobey. "TV Sports: The Next Dimension." Popular Mechanics 1 Mar.
29        1998, p. 69.

30    Briggs, John. "The Promise of Virtual Reality." The Futurist 1 Sept. 1996.

31    Hargrave, Sean. "Fighting Crime in 3-D mode." The Toronto Star 28 Feb. 1999.

**GO ON** ➡

**1** What is the **BEST** way to rewrite the main idea statement in lines 3–4? ("*In fact…in medicine.*")

  **A** In fact, researchers think this exciting new technology can change education.

  **B** Virtual reality is changing the ways researchers look at how police do their jobs.

  **C** In fact, researchers are discovering many practical uses for this exciting technology.

  **D** Medicine is using research in the field of virtual reality to train doctors and students.

**2** What is the **BEST** way to improve the organization of Paragraph 2 (lines 5–9)?

  **F** Move the first sentence to the end of the paragraph

  **G** Delete the second sentence

  **H** Delete the third sentence

  **J** Move the last sentence to the beginning of the paragraph

**3** What is the **BEST** way to rewrite the sentences in lines 10–12? ("*Virtual reality … real patients.*")

  **A** To help doctors practice surgery and other risky procedures without jeopardizing real patients, doctors use virtual reality.

  **B** Virtual reality helping doctors learn how to do surgery and other risky procedures without jeopardizing real patients.

  **C** Virtual reality helps doctors do their jobs better by helping them practice surgery.

  **D** Risky procedures and surgery, by using virtual reality, doctors can practice with it without jeopardizing real patients.

**4** What is the **BEST** change, if any, to add variety to the sentences in lines 14–16? ("*Police in … took place.*")

  **F** To look at crime scenes in a new way, police in England are experimenting with a virtual reality system.

  **G** Police in England, to look at crime scenes in a new way, are experimenting with a virtual reality system.

  **H** Police in England are experimenting with looking at crimes a new way with virtual reality.

  **J** Make no change

**5** What is the **BEST** change, if any, to make to improve the organization of Paragraph 4?

  **A** Add a main idea statement

  **B** Delete the first sentence

  **C** Delete the last sentence

  **D** Make no change

**6** What is the **BEST** change, if any, to add variety to the sentence in lines 20–23? ("*A viewer… the players.*")

  **F** A viewer can use a new program called Virtual Replay to look at the play.

  **G** A viewer can use a new program called Virtual Replay to recreate the playing field, the play, and the players inside a computer.

  **H** To fabricate the field and calculate the whereabouts of the players, a viewer can use a new computer program called Virtual Replay.

  **J** Make no change

**GO ON**

**7** What is the **BEST** change, if any, to make to the sentence in lines 23–25? (*"In the ... replay regularly."*)

  **A** In the past, a referee, who used instant replay, could decide whether or not a call was correct.

  **B** A referee, who would not be limited to just a couple of camera angles, could use Virtual Replay to decide whether or not a call was correct.

  **C** A referee, who called plays with instant replay could get the same results with Virtual Replay.

  **D** Make no change

**8** What is the **BEST** way to improve the conclusion of the essay (line 26)?

  **F** Add a sentence that catches the reader's interest

  **G** Include more facts and statistics

  **H** Restate the report's main idea

  **J** Refer to the number of sources you have used

**9** What is the **BEST** change, if any, to make to all the entries in the Works Cited in lines 27–31?

  **A** Remove the underlines

  **B** Delete the periods after the authors' names

  **C** Put the entries in alphabetical order

  **D** Make no change

**10** What is the **BEST** change, if any, to make to the first entry in the Works Cited in lines 28–29? (*"Grumet, Tobey... 69."*)

  **F** Underline Popular Mechanics

  **G** Delete the quotation marks

  **H** Change *Grumet, Tobey* to **Tobey Grumet**

  **J** Make no change

# Reading Workshop: Persuasive Article

**DIRECTIONS** *You have probably seen articles in local newspapers in which writers express views either for or against something. Here the mother of a middle school student gives her views on soft-drink vending machines in the school. Read the following passage to find out whether she is for or against them and why.*

Dear Principal Llanes:

I have been a strong supporter of Bartow Middle School for many years. I am concerned, however, by the school's recent decision to place soda machines in the cafeteria. I do not believe that schools should encourage students to buy and drink soda.

First, soda is not a healthful drink. Most 12-ounce cans of soda contain about 10 teaspoonfuls of sugar. Nutrition expert Michael Jacobson says, "Soda pop is junk." He points out in his book *Liquid Candy* that the sugar in soft drinks can lead to many problems, including obesity and tooth decay. In addition, soda contains absolutely no vitamins or minerals. Students who drink soda instead of milk or juice are missing out on vital nutrients.

Encouraging students to make healthy choices about nutrition is more important than ever. Students today are more overweight than they have ever been. In 1963, only 15 percent of American children and teenagers were overweight. That number is now between 31 and 37 percent. Clearly, students do not need more fattening drinks with no nutritional value. In fact, students now drink twice as much soda as they do milk. Twenty years ago, students drank twice as much milk as they do today. Consequently, many teeenagers are now suffering from a lack of calcium. This affects bone growth and quality. Studies show that lack of calcium makes bones more prone to fractures and increases the risk of bone disease later in life. Clearly, our young people do not need the empty calories from soda, but they do need the nutrients from healthful drinks.

Giving students the option of buying soda at school encourages poor nutrition. My daughter is in the seventh grade at Bartow Middle School. Even though I have stressed the importance of good nutrition, she tells me that she often buys soda at school instead of milk. She says her friends do the same. Without the soda machines in the cafeteria, these students would be choosing milk, juice, or water, all healthier options than soda.

Besides the health aspects of this issue, I am concerned about our students being bombarded by free advertising. Soda machines, with their brightly colored logos, are free billboards in the cafeteria. Would we let a popular shoe manufacturer put up a billboard in the school? It is not the school's place to advertise, but that is exactly what the school does by approving these machines. Taxpayers give free and continuous advertising to a product that, in many ways, is unhealthful.

I realize that the school earns a large profit from these machines. However, we should not compromise our young people's health for the sake of a dollar. Please remove the soda machines from the cafeteria so that Bartow Middle School can be a place that educates students in positive, healthful ways.

Sincerely,

Kiera Saunders

1. How can you tell that this passage is persuasive?

   A It is written in the form of a letter to someone in charge.

   B It is only one person's point of view.

   C It uses examples that illustrate important ideas.

   D It offers an opinion and supports it with reasons and evidence.

2. Which of the following is the author's point of view in this passage?

   A Schools should promote physical education.

   B Students make poor choices about nutrition.

   C Bartow Middle School needs to offer better nutrition.

   D Soda machines do not belong in school cafeterias.

3. What main issue does the author address in paragraph 3?

   A advertising directed at teenagers

   B teens' nutritional needs

   C young people on diets

   D empty calories in soda

4. Why does the author point out that students now drink twice as much soda as milk?

   A as evidence for a reason

   B as a main reason

   C as an anecdote

   D as a summary

5. What kind of evidence does the following statement use: "In 1963, only 15 percent of American children and teenagers were overweight"?

   A fact

   B anecdote

   C expert point of view

   D opinion statement

6. Why does the author include the quote by Michael Jacobson?

   A to show support from other parents

   B to provide an expert opinion as evidence

   C to provide an emotional appeal

   D to give a student's opinion

7. In paragraph 5, what point of view does the author express?

   A Schools should accept only paid advertising.

   B Schools benefit from free advertising.

   C Schools should not support advertising.

   D Advertising teaches students to be better consumers.

8. Why does the author mention her daughter in the fourth paragraph?

   A to make an emotional appeal

   B to identify the issue

   C to use an anecdote as evidence

   D to show student support on the issue

9. In the last paragraph, why does the author include statements about profits?

   A to reveal that soda companies do not care about good health

   B to emphasize that good health is more valuable than money

   C to offer a solution to a problem

   D to address counterarguments

10. What action does the author want the principal to take?

    A offer only milk for lunch

    B sell soda only at the lunch counter

    C ban soda from the school grounds

    D take out the soda machines

# Writing Workshop: Persuasive Essay

**DIRECTIONS** The passage that follows is an early draft of a student essay. Some parts need to be rewritten. Read the passage and select the best answers for the questions that follow. Some questions are about particular sentences and ask you to improve sentence structure and word choice. Other questions refer to parts of the essay and ask you to consider organization and development. In making your decision, follow the conventions of standard written English. After you have chosen your answer, fill in the corresponding oval on your answer sheet.

*(1) Over the summer, I visited my cousin in another state. (2) When she asked me if I wanted to see her yearbook, I said, "Sure!" (3) She promptly popped a DVD into the player, and I watched a yearbook full of color, action, interviews, and music. (4) There are some pros and cons about video yearbooks for Northside Middle School students to consider.*

*(5) Video does a completer job of portraying people and events than still photography. (6) My cousin's yearbook captured the band playing the school fight song. (7) No print yearbook can do that. (8) Video also allows viewers to see a more big picture of an event. (9) Suppose the basketball team gets carried away. (10) A video yearbook can capture the sound of the buzzer, the roar of the crowd, and the happy celebrating of the team. (11) Print yearbooks just cannot compete with moving pictures and sound to capture excitement and emotion.*

*(12) The cost of printing continues to rise, but the cost of technology is decreasing. (13) Northside's yearbook with 56 pages cost $28.00. (14) Overtown Middle School's video yearbook cost $20.00. (15) Students and parents both like to save money.*

*(16) Producing a video yearbook also teaches students how to put their best foot forward with technology. (17) Students learn how to film, edit, and use graphics to make an effective video. (18) Mike Gieger, president of Gieger Enterprises, says, "Multimedia presentations are becoming more important in business all the time. (19) My employees need to know how to use this technology." (20) Producing a video yearbook would give students an opportunity to learn these multimedia skills.*

*(21) A print yearbook may soon be as outdated as a typewriter. (22) After all, it is hard to compete against a popular video yearbook.*

1. For the purpose of grabbing the audience's attention, which of the following represents the best revision of sentence 1?

   (A) My cousin had a surprise for me.
   (B) My cousin had something to share with me.
   (C) Over the summer, I got a good idea from my cousin.
   (D) My cousin couldn't wait to get me into the TV room.

2. Which of the following represents the best revision of sentence 4?

   (A) Northside Middle School needs to improve its print yearbook.
   (B) Northside Middle School students need to consider what kind of yearbook they want.
   (C) One option for Northside Middle School is to produce both a video and print yearbook.
   (D) Northside Middle School should produce a video yearbook instead of a print yearbook.

3.  What represents the best revision of sentence 5?

    (A) Video does a more complete job of portraying people and events than still photography.

    (B) Video does a completer job of portraying people and events.

    (C) Video is completer at portraying people and events than still photography does.

    (D) Video does a job of portraying people and events than still photography.

4.  Which of the following represents the best revision of sentence 8?

    (A) Video also allows viewers to see a more bigger picture of an event.

    (B) Video also allows viewers to see a more big picture of an event.

    (C) A most big picture is allowed viewers by an events video.

    (D) Video also allows viewers to see a bigger picture of an event.

5.  Which is the best revision of sentence 9?

    (A) Suppose the basketball team takes a back seat.

    (B) Suppose the basketball team hits the nail on the head.

    (C) Suppose the basketball team shakes a leg.

    (D) Suppose the basketball team wins the tournament.

6.  Which of the following sentences would best serve as a reason in the third paragraph?

    (A) Video yearbooks also cost less than print yearbooks.

    (B) Video yearbooks have more appeal than print yearbooks.

    (C) Print yearbooks are becoming too old-fashioned.

    (D) Students can use equipment that Northside already has.

7.  Which of the following represents the best revision of sentence 16?

    (A) Producing a video yearbook also teaches students how to sink or swim with technology.

    (B) Producing a video yearbook also teaches students how to climb the ladder of success with technology.

    (C) Producing a video yearbook also teaches students how to communicate effectively with technology.

    (D) Producing a video yearbook also teaches students how to come through with flying colors with technology.

8.  What is the function of sentences 18 and 19?

    (A) To provide factual support.

    (B) To include an anecdote.

    (C) To summarize reasons.

    (D) To provide an expert opinion.

**GO ON**

9. Which of the following represents the best revision of sentence 22 as a summary of reasons?

   (A) After all, it is hard to argue with what all the other middle schools in our district are already doing with their yearbooks.

   (B) After all, it is hard to argue with a yearbook that teaches students discipline, sports, and technology.

   (C) After all, it is hard to argue with an action-packed and inexpensive yearbook that teaches students important skills.

   (D) After all, it is hard to argue with my cousin and the success and popularity that the video yearbook has had at her school.

10. What does the conclusion of the essay need in order to be complete?

   (A) A familiar cliché.

   (B) Restatement of opinion.

   (C) Persuasive techniques.

   (D) Statistical evidence.

# Reading Workshop: Print Advertisement

**DIRECTIONS** Read the advertisement. Then read each question that follows the advertisement. Decide which is the best answer to each question. Mark the letter for that answer.

## Remember when you wanted to be a superhero?

### *Become a volunteer and you will be!*

Volunteers are heroes. They may not fly faster than a speeding bullet, but volunteers change lives. They feed the hungry, help kids with their homework, clean up neighborhood parks, take care of abandoned animals, and visit the elderly. Your school has a volunteer service coordinator who will help you find the place where you can be a superhero. Many other students are already volunteering — why not join them? You will discover what they already know: you don't need a red cape or special powers to be a superhero. All you really need is a heart. Call 1-800-555-1234 to get more information about joining the Youth Volunteer Service Corps.

**GO ON** →

1   What generalization does the creator of the headline probably want the reader to make?

   **A** Children like to wear superhero costumes.

   **B** Volunteers usually like children in costumes.

   **C** At some time, most children have looked up to superheroes.

   **D** At one time, volunteers were considered to be superheroes.

2   When the ad refers to the other students who are volunteering, it is using —

   **F** a faulty generalization

   **G** a testimonial

   **H** clue words

   **J** the bandwagon technique

3   What generalization does the writer of the ad probably want the reader to make?

   **A** People who become volunteers are special.

   **B** The volunteer service coordinator needs help.

   **C** People who are not volunteers are selfish.

   **D** People become volunteers to get attention.

4   This ad is using persuasive techniques to —

   **F** make faulty generalizations

   **G** influence people in a negative way

   **H** convince students to volunteer

   **J** deceive the public

5   Based on this ad, what generalization could you make about the Youth Volunteer Service Corps?

   **A** Young children who want to become superheroes have joined.

   **B** Its volunteers are doing important work.

   **C** It recruits only the smartest, most talented students in school.

   **D** It needs money more than it needs volunteers.

6   Which statement summarizes the emotional appeal of the ad?

   **F** The ad appeals to negative emotions.

   **G** The ad appeals to positive emotions.

   **H** The ad does not use an emotional appeal.

   **J** The emotional appeal is only in the ad's image.

7   What is the ad specifically trying to persuade the reader to do?

   **A** Help children become superheroes

   **B** Find a place to buy a superhero cape

   **C** Make new friends

   **D** Join the Youth Volunteer Service Corps

8   What logical support does the ad provide to persuade the reader?

   **F** It lists the work volunteers do to make a difference.

   **G** It gives the toll-free number of the Youth Volunteer Service Corps.

   **H** It makes the reader feel good about joining the organization.

   **J** It says that volunteers are heroes.

9   The statement that all a person needs is a heart in order to volunteer suggests that —

   **A** all volunteers are in good physical condition

   **B** volunteers are concerned with the well-being of others

   **C** students care only if they join the Youth Volunteer Service Corps

   **D** volunteers mainly assist people with medical problems

10  This ad is trying to get its readers to feel —

   **F** excited about becoming a volunteer

   **G** good about students who are helping the community

   **H** embarrassed about the needs in the community

   **J** too busy to volunteer

# Writing Workshop: Print Advertisement

**DIRECTIONS** *The following ad was created by a student for the local newspaper. Read the ad (which may contain some errors) and answer the questions that follow. Be sure to fill in the bubble next to the answer you choose. Mark like this ◉ not like this ⊘ . You may look back at the ad as you answer the questions.*

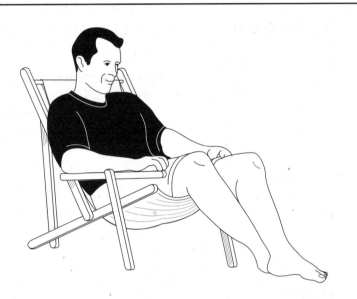

1   # Take a fun ride!

2   Is summer vacation boring already? Come to WaterWorks for an exciting
3   time! Climb Thunder Tower, where you will drop straight down our big
4   slide. Hang on as you go through River Rapids aboard one of our five-
5   person rafts. When you need to dry out, our beachs warm sands will help
6   you catch a few rays while you chat with your friends. You can count on
7   seeing them there because everyone knows that WaterWorks is the only
8   place for major summer fun. Take advantage of WaterWorks extended
9   summer hours.

10   ## WaterWorks
11   **1902 Hartland Road**
12   **555-3338**

**GO ON ➡**

NAME _____ CLASS _____ DATE _____

for **CHAPTER 26**  page 728  continued

**2** Which of the following changes should be made to the ad's artwork?

○ Show the person eating a slice of pizza

○ Change the adult to a small child

○ Show a teenager riding an exciting ride

○ Show a picture of a lifeguard

**2** Which of the following slogans is preferable to *Take a fun ride*? (line 1)

○ Come to WaterWorks for summer fun!

○ Our lifeguards will keep you safe!

○ Families love our rides!

○ Take a ride on the wild side!

**3** Which of the following sentences is preferable to the one beginning, *Is summer vacation...* in line 2?

○ Has summer vacation become old already?

○ Are you too old for summer?

○ Do you find summer vacation getting old?

○ Are you getting bored with your summer vacation?

**4** Which of the following sentences is preferable to the one beginning, *Come to WaterWorks ...* in lines 2–3?

○ Come to WaterWorks to surf, sun, eat, and chat with your friends!

○ Then come on down to WaterWorks for a rip-roaring, spine-tingling, surfing adventure!

○ WaterWorks offers many fun water rides that people of all ages enjoy!

○ Teens love the exciting and fun rides they find at WaterWorks!

**5** In the sentence, *Climb Thunder Tower, where you will drop straight down our big slide.*, which of the following changes would improve the emotional appeal of the sentence? (lines 3–4)

○ Change **drop** to **descend**

○ Change **drop** to **coast**

○ Change **big** to **huge**

○ Change **big** to **monster**

**6** In the sentence, *Hang on as you go through River Rapids aboard one of our five-person rafts.*, which of the following changes would improve the sentence? (lines 4–5)

○ Change **hang** to **hold**

○ Change **go** to **rock**

○ Change **aboard** to **on**

○ Change **rafts** to **boats**

**7** In the sentence, *When you need to dry out, our beachs warm sands will help you catch a few rays while you chat with your friends.*, which of the following changes should be made? (lines 5–6)

○ Change **beachs** to **beach's**

○ Change **beachs** to **beaches**

○ Change **sands** to **sands'**

○ Change **rays** to **ray's**

**8** Which of the following facts should be included in the ad?

○ the average number of people who visit the park

○ the number of training hours the lifeguards receive

○ the cost of a hamburger at one of the concession stands

○ the opening and closing times of the new hours

**GO ON** ➡

**76**      ELEMENTS OF LANGUAGE | First Course | *Chapter Tests in Standardized Test Formats*

**9** In the sentence, *Take advantage of WaterWorks extended summer hours.,* which of the following changes should be made? (lines 8–9)

- ○ Change **WaterWorks** to **WaterWork's**
- ○ Change **WaterWorks** to **WaterWorks'**
- ○ Change **WaterWorks** to **WaterWorks's**
- ○ Change **WaterWorks** to **Water's Work**

**10** Which of the following sentences should be added to the end of the text to clarify what the reader should do?

- ○ To apply for a lifeguard position, call our employment office at 555-3342.
- ○ You can make special music requests by calling one of the WaterWorks' deejays at 555-3344.
- ○ Don't let the lazy days of summer find you watching TV all day.
- ○ So come on and catch a wave this summer at WaterWorks.

*Most standardized tests require that you use a No. 2 pencil. Each mark should be dark and completely fill the intended oval. Be sure to completely erase any errors or stray marks. If you do not have a pencil, follow your teacher's instructions about how to mark your answers on this sheet.*

**2 Your Name**

| First 4 Letters of Last Name | | | | First Init. | Mid. Init. |
|---|---|---|---|---|---|
| Ⓐ | Ⓐ | Ⓐ | Ⓐ | Ⓐ | Ⓐ |
| Ⓑ | Ⓑ | Ⓑ | Ⓑ | Ⓑ | Ⓑ |
| Ⓒ | Ⓒ | Ⓒ | Ⓒ | Ⓒ | Ⓒ |
| Ⓓ | Ⓓ | Ⓓ | Ⓓ | Ⓓ | Ⓓ |
| Ⓔ | Ⓔ | Ⓔ | Ⓔ | Ⓔ | Ⓔ |
| Ⓕ | Ⓕ | Ⓕ | Ⓕ | Ⓕ | Ⓕ |
| Ⓖ | Ⓖ | Ⓖ | Ⓖ | Ⓖ | Ⓖ |
| Ⓗ | Ⓗ | Ⓗ | Ⓗ | Ⓗ | Ⓗ |
| Ⓘ | Ⓘ | Ⓘ | Ⓘ | Ⓘ | Ⓘ |
| Ⓙ | Ⓙ | Ⓙ | Ⓙ | Ⓙ | Ⓙ |
| Ⓚ | Ⓚ | Ⓚ | Ⓚ | Ⓚ | Ⓚ |
| Ⓛ | Ⓛ | Ⓛ | Ⓛ | Ⓛ | Ⓛ |
| Ⓜ | Ⓜ | Ⓜ | Ⓜ | Ⓜ | Ⓜ |
| Ⓝ | Ⓝ | Ⓝ | Ⓝ | Ⓝ | Ⓝ |
| Ⓞ | Ⓞ | Ⓞ | Ⓞ | Ⓞ | Ⓞ |
| Ⓟ | Ⓟ | Ⓟ | Ⓟ | Ⓟ | Ⓟ |
| Ⓠ | Ⓠ | Ⓠ | Ⓠ | Ⓠ | Ⓠ |
| Ⓡ | Ⓡ | Ⓡ | Ⓡ | Ⓡ | Ⓡ |
| Ⓢ | Ⓢ | Ⓢ | Ⓢ | Ⓢ | Ⓢ |
| Ⓣ | Ⓣ | Ⓣ | Ⓣ | Ⓣ | Ⓣ |
| Ⓤ | Ⓤ | Ⓤ | Ⓤ | Ⓤ | Ⓤ |
| Ⓥ | Ⓥ | Ⓥ | Ⓥ | Ⓥ | Ⓥ |
| Ⓦ | Ⓦ | Ⓦ | Ⓦ | Ⓦ | Ⓦ |
| Ⓧ | Ⓧ | Ⓧ | Ⓧ | Ⓧ | Ⓧ |
| Ⓨ | Ⓨ | Ⓨ | Ⓨ | Ⓨ | Ⓨ |
| Ⓩ | Ⓩ | Ⓩ | Ⓩ | Ⓩ | Ⓩ |

**1**

Your Name: _____
(Print)        Last                          First                          M.I.

Signature: _____

Class: _____  Date: ___ / ___ / ___
(Print)                                              Month  Day  Year

**3 Date**

| Month | | Day | | Year | |
|---|---|---|---|---|---|
| Jan. ◯ | | | | | |
| Feb. ◯ | | | | | |
| Mar. ◯ | ⓪ | ⓪ | ⓪ | ⓪ | |
| Apr. ◯ | ① | ① | ① | ① | |
| May ◯ | ② | ② | ② | ② | |
| June ◯ | ③ | ③ | ③ | ③ | |
| July ◯ | | ④ | ④ | ④ | |
| Aug. ◯ | | ⑤ | ⑤ | ⑤ | |
| Sept. ◯ | | ⑥ | ⑥ | ⑥ | |
| Oct. ◯ | | ⑦ | ⑦ | ⑦ | |
| Nov. ◯ | | ⑧ | ⑧ | ⑧ | |
| Dec. ◯ | | ⑨ | ⑨ | ⑨ | |

**4 Grade**

| | |
|---|---|
| ⓪ | ⓪ |
| ① | ① |
| | ② |
| | ③ |
| | ④ |
| | ⑤ |
| | ⑥ |
| | ⑦ |
| | ⑧ |
| | ⑨ |

**5 Age**

| | |
|---|---|
| ⓪ | ⓪ |
| ① | ① |
| | ② |
| | ③ |
| | ④ |
| | ⑤ |
| | ⑥ |
| | ⑦ |
| | ⑧ |
| | ⑨ |

*For each new section, begin with number 1. If a section has more answer spaces than questions, leave the extra spaces blank.*

**Grammar and Usage Test**

Section **1**
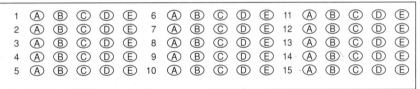

Section **2**

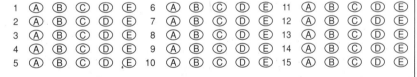

**Mechanics Test**

Section **1**

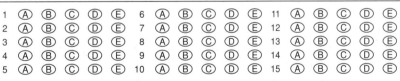

Section **2**

# Answer Sheet 1

## Chapter_____

## Grammar, Usage, and Mechanics

1  Ⓐ  Ⓑ  Ⓒ  Ⓓ
2  Ⓐ  Ⓑ  Ⓒ  Ⓓ
3  Ⓐ  Ⓑ  Ⓒ  Ⓓ
4  Ⓐ  Ⓑ  Ⓒ  Ⓓ
5  Ⓐ  Ⓑ  Ⓒ  Ⓓ
6  Ⓐ  Ⓑ  Ⓒ  Ⓓ
7  Ⓐ  Ⓑ  Ⓒ  Ⓓ
8  Ⓐ  Ⓑ  Ⓒ  Ⓓ
9  Ⓐ  Ⓑ  Ⓒ  Ⓓ
10 Ⓐ  Ⓑ  Ⓒ  Ⓓ

# Answer Sheet 2

# Chapter_____

## Sentences and Paragraphs

| | | | | | | | | | | |
|---|---|---|---|---|---|---|---|---|---|---|
| 1 | Ⓐ | Ⓑ | Ⓒ | Ⓓ | | 11 | Ⓐ | Ⓑ | Ⓒ | Ⓓ |
| 2 | Ⓕ | Ⓖ | Ⓗ | Ⓙ | | 12 | Ⓕ | Ⓖ | Ⓗ | Ⓙ |
| 3 | Ⓐ | Ⓑ | Ⓒ | Ⓓ | | 13 | Ⓐ | Ⓑ | Ⓒ | Ⓓ |
| 4 | Ⓕ | Ⓖ | Ⓗ | Ⓙ | | 14 | Ⓕ | Ⓖ | Ⓗ | Ⓙ |
| 5 | Ⓐ | Ⓑ | Ⓒ | Ⓓ | | 15 | Ⓐ | Ⓑ | Ⓒ | Ⓓ |
| 6 | Ⓕ | Ⓖ | Ⓗ | Ⓙ | | 16 | Ⓕ | Ⓖ | Ⓗ | Ⓙ |
| 7 | Ⓐ | Ⓑ | Ⓒ | Ⓓ | | 17 | Ⓐ | Ⓑ | Ⓒ | Ⓓ |
| 8 | Ⓕ | Ⓖ | Ⓗ | Ⓙ | | 18 | Ⓕ | Ⓖ | Ⓗ | Ⓙ |
| 9 | Ⓐ | Ⓑ | Ⓒ | Ⓓ | | 19 | Ⓐ | Ⓑ | Ⓒ | Ⓓ |
| 10 | Ⓕ | Ⓖ | Ⓗ | Ⓙ | | 20 | Ⓕ | Ⓖ | Ⓗ | Ⓙ |

# Answer Sheet 3

## Chapter_____

## Sentences and Paragraphs

| | | | | | | | | | |
|---|---|---|---|---|---|---|---|---|---|
| 1 | Ⓐ | Ⓑ | Ⓒ | Ⓓ | 11 | Ⓐ | Ⓑ | Ⓒ | Ⓓ |
| 2 | Ⓐ | Ⓑ | Ⓒ | Ⓓ | 12 | Ⓐ | Ⓑ | Ⓒ | Ⓓ |
| 3 | Ⓐ | Ⓑ | Ⓒ | Ⓓ | 13 | Ⓐ | Ⓑ | Ⓒ | Ⓓ |
| 4 | Ⓐ | Ⓑ | Ⓒ | Ⓓ | 14 | Ⓐ | Ⓑ | Ⓒ | Ⓓ |
| 5 | Ⓐ | Ⓑ | Ⓒ | Ⓓ | 15 | Ⓐ | Ⓑ | Ⓒ | Ⓓ |
| 6 | Ⓐ | Ⓑ | Ⓒ | Ⓓ | 16 | Ⓐ | Ⓑ | Ⓒ | Ⓓ |
| 7 | Ⓐ | Ⓑ | Ⓒ | Ⓓ | 17 | Ⓐ | Ⓑ | Ⓒ | Ⓓ |
| 8 | Ⓐ | Ⓑ | Ⓒ | Ⓓ | 18 | Ⓐ | Ⓑ | Ⓒ | Ⓓ |
| 9 | Ⓐ | Ⓑ | Ⓒ | Ⓓ | 19 | Ⓐ | Ⓑ | Ⓒ | Ⓓ |
| 10 | Ⓐ | Ⓑ | Ⓒ | Ⓓ | 20 | Ⓐ | Ⓑ | Ⓒ | Ⓓ |

*Chapter Tests in Standardized Test Formats*

# Answer Sheet 4

## Chapter_____

## Reading Workshop

| | | | | | | | | | | | | |
|---|---|---|---|---|---|---|---|---|---|---|---|---|
| 1 | Ⓐ Ⓑ Ⓒ Ⓓ | | 5 | Ⓐ Ⓑ Ⓒ Ⓓ | | 9 | Ⓐ Ⓑ Ⓒ Ⓓ |
| 2 | Ⓕ Ⓖ Ⓗ Ⓙ | | 6 | Ⓕ Ⓖ Ⓗ Ⓙ | | 10 | Ⓕ Ⓖ Ⓗ Ⓙ |
| 3 | Ⓐ Ⓑ Ⓒ Ⓓ | | 7 | Ⓐ Ⓑ Ⓒ Ⓓ |
| 4 | Ⓕ Ⓖ Ⓗ Ⓙ | | 8 | Ⓕ Ⓖ Ⓗ Ⓙ |

## Writing Workshop

| | | | | | | | | | | | | |
|---|---|---|---|---|---|---|---|---|---|---|---|---|
| 1 | Ⓐ Ⓑ Ⓒ Ⓓ | | 5 | Ⓐ Ⓑ Ⓒ Ⓓ | | 9 | Ⓐ Ⓑ Ⓒ Ⓓ |
| 2 | Ⓕ Ⓖ Ⓗ Ⓙ | | 6 | Ⓕ Ⓖ Ⓗ Ⓙ | | 10 | Ⓕ Ⓖ Ⓗ Ⓙ |
| 3 | Ⓐ Ⓑ Ⓒ Ⓓ | | 7 | Ⓐ Ⓑ Ⓒ Ⓓ |
| 4 | Ⓕ Ⓖ Ⓗ Ⓙ | | 8 | Ⓕ Ⓖ Ⓗ Ⓙ |

# Answer Sheet 5

# Chapter_____

---

## Reading Workshop

| 1 | Ⓐ Ⓑ Ⓒ Ⓓ | 5 | Ⓐ Ⓑ Ⓒ Ⓓ | 9 | Ⓐ Ⓑ Ⓒ Ⓓ |
|---|---|---|---|---|---|
| 2 | Ⓕ Ⓖ Ⓗ Ⓘ | 6 | Ⓕ Ⓖ Ⓗ Ⓘ | 10 | Ⓕ Ⓖ Ⓗ Ⓘ |
| 3 | Ⓐ Ⓑ Ⓒ Ⓓ | 7 | Ⓐ Ⓑ Ⓒ Ⓓ | | |
| 4 | Ⓕ Ⓖ Ⓗ Ⓘ | 8 | Ⓕ Ⓖ Ⓗ Ⓘ | | |

---

## Writing Workshop

| 1 | Ⓐ Ⓑ Ⓒ Ⓓ | 5 | Ⓐ Ⓑ Ⓒ Ⓓ | 9 | Ⓐ Ⓑ Ⓒ Ⓓ |
|---|---|---|---|---|---|
| 2 | Ⓕ Ⓖ Ⓗ Ⓘ | 6 | Ⓕ Ⓖ Ⓗ Ⓘ | 10 | Ⓕ Ⓖ Ⓗ Ⓘ |
| 3 | Ⓐ Ⓑ Ⓒ Ⓓ | 7 | Ⓐ Ⓑ Ⓒ Ⓓ | | |
| 4 | Ⓕ Ⓖ Ⓗ Ⓘ | 8 | Ⓕ Ⓖ Ⓗ Ⓘ | | |

# Answer Sheet 6

## Chapter _____

---

## Reading Workshop

| 1 | Ⓐ Ⓑ Ⓒ Ⓓ | 5 | Ⓐ Ⓑ Ⓒ Ⓓ | 9 | Ⓐ Ⓑ Ⓒ Ⓓ |
|---|---|---|---|---|---|
| 2 | Ⓐ Ⓑ Ⓒ Ⓓ | 6 | Ⓐ Ⓑ Ⓒ Ⓓ | 10 | Ⓐ Ⓑ Ⓒ Ⓓ |
| 3 | Ⓐ Ⓑ Ⓒ Ⓓ | 7 | Ⓐ Ⓑ Ⓒ Ⓓ | | |
| 4 | Ⓐ Ⓑ Ⓒ Ⓓ | 8 | Ⓐ Ⓑ Ⓒ Ⓓ | | |

---

## Writing Workshop

| 1 | Ⓐ Ⓑ Ⓒ Ⓓ | 5 | Ⓐ Ⓑ Ⓒ Ⓓ | 9 | Ⓐ Ⓑ Ⓒ Ⓓ |
|---|---|---|---|---|---|
| 2 | Ⓐ Ⓑ Ⓒ Ⓓ | 6 | Ⓐ Ⓑ Ⓒ Ⓓ | 10 | Ⓐ Ⓑ Ⓒ Ⓓ |
| 3 | Ⓐ Ⓑ Ⓒ Ⓓ | 7 | Ⓐ Ⓑ Ⓒ Ⓓ | | |
| 4 | Ⓐ Ⓑ Ⓒ Ⓓ | 8 | Ⓐ Ⓑ Ⓒ Ⓓ | | |

# Notes

# Notes

# Notes